The Richard Prangley Story

Waiting for Home

A True Story of Strength and Survival

Richard L. Prangley

THE RICHARD PRANGLEY STORY

Waiting for Home

A TRUE STORY OF STRENGTH AND SURVIVAL

John Schneider

William B. Eerdmans Publishing Company
Grand Rapids, Michigan/Cambridge, U.K.

© 1998 Wm B. Eerdmans Publishing Co.

255 Jefferson Ave. SE., Grand Rapids, Michigan 49503 /
P.O. Box 163, Cambridge CB3 9PU U.K.

Printed in the United States of America

02 01 00 99 98   7 6 5 4 3 2 1

Library of Congress Cataloging-in-Publication Data

Schneider, John, 1949-
Waiting for home : the Richard Prangley story / John Schneider.
    p.   cm.
ISBN 0-8028-4211-9 (alk. paper)
1. Prangley, Richard, 1949-   . 2. Mentally handicapped —
United States — Biography. 3. Mentally handicapped —
Institutional care — United States. I. Title.
HV3006.A39P737   1998
362.3'092
[B] — DC21   97-31904
                                                              CIP

Table of Contents

For the Richard Prangleys everywhere

Foreword

Any characterization of Richard Prangley has to start with dreams, hope, faith, determination and inspiration. More than anything else, though, what characterizes Richard is his constant yearning for independence.

Richard is a victim of family loss and ostracism. He was labeled retarded, separated from his family at age 6 and institutionalized. He has known the meaning of stigma and bias. He has felt the scorn of prejudice and remains scarred but not broken. He carries no animosity for what he has experienced and endured. A man of faith, he has been sustained in adversity by his belief in God and the resurrection. Richard clearly understands forgiveness, for he practices it with his family, with those who have hurt him in the past, and with those who discriminate against him now. He cradles an intrinsic desire to make life better for others. As long as I have known Richard, he has talked about telling his story so that we can better understand the past in order to change the future. The time for his story has come! And the author of this book, John Schneider, brings a special sensitivity to the telling of it.

Richard spent 15 years (1956–71) in the Coldwater State Home and Training School, an institution that was closed in 1985. In the era when he lived at Coldwater, many people who had a developmental disability lived their entire lives in a state-operated institution. Richard lived that institutional life. He learned the daily institutional routine. His home was a cottage with a number and no name. His siblings were his dorm mates; his father figure, the facility superintendent. His schooling and work experience were basically working the fields of the institution's truck farms. For some at Coldwater, to say that they have experienced life would be a stretch of faith. For Richard, it is evident that fully experiencing life in every way beyond custodial care was, for him, never a question of whether — only of when.

Richard's life today stands in sharp contrast to his initial path. He now works in the Office Services Division of the Michigan Department of Community Health. He has worked for the State of Michigan since 1980. True to his Dutch roots, Richard expects to give a full day's work for his pay. He is always punctual, conscientious in every task and incapable of loafing. Though he does not know how to read, he is valued for his experience, his knowledge of where things are and how to get things done, and his ability to make otherwise mundane tasks go quickly and easily. Richard is proud of his contribution to the everyday workings of the department.

The result of Richard's perseverance is a life of abundant dimensions. He enjoys collecting photos and other memorabilia and displaying them in his apartment. He loves baseball and cherishes his tickets to the Lansing Lugnuts games, the local minor league baseball team. Movies, concerts, shopping, traveling on long weekends, and dinner with friends and colleagues are among his leisure activities. Life does not pass him by.

The first thing that one realizes about Richard is his commitment to independence — his own and that of others who have a developmental disability or mental illness. It is a commitment of conscience, a burning and abiding passion. It is his mission, and he lives it and articulates it with the zeal of an ardent revivalist. As Richard works to turn around people's perceptions and attitudes about those who have a disability, his accomplishments — in both his work life and his advocacy — and his story are an inspiration. Richard is living proof that the key to supporting developmentally disabled persons in their own communities — not in institutions or dependent housing — is self-determination.

Richard is effective in his role as an advocate for community-based care, which is now one of the cornerstones of Michigan's extensive community mental health system. His efforts led to preparation of the Mental Health Educational Exhibit, which has traveled throughout the state, educating schoolchildren, consumers of mental health services and their families, and the general public about the progress that Michigan has made in mental health care.

When we worked with the state legislature to rewrite Michigan's Mental Health Code, we focused on consumer choice, self-determination, people-first language and a host of other updates to enhance services for consumers and their families. Often, the experiences that Richard brought into our lives were in our hearts as we approached the milestone legislation.

Richard's tenacity has aided him in winning the admiration and respect of scores of state employees, four Mental Health Department directors and three governors — including Gov. John Engler — in his odyssey to independence. His winning smile and twinkling eyes continue to convey his faith in people and his sense of humor in facing whatever life brings his way.

For me, Richard has been a friend, a mentor and a partner as we work together to revitalize and redirect health services in Michigan. I remember the day in 1996, when the Department of Mental Health, after consolidating with several other departments, was renamed the Michigan Department of Community Health. Richard ran into my office early that morning, after he had heard it on the radio, and said, "We did it; we did it!" When I asked him what we did, Richard said, "We finally got rid of that word *mental* — it's a stigma word!"

Richard's optimism and unconditional love are contagious. Knowing Richard is to know that today one can stand against the cold wind and rain believing that tomorrow, or the next day, you will be able to sit in the sun and smile.

James K. Haveman Jr., director
Michigan Department of Community Health

The Arrival

I know I always made my mother nervous — I could feel it. I tried to play with other kids on my street, but it never worked out. I don't know why — it just never worked out. I guess I was a handful. I guess I was a real pistol.
— Richard Prangley

Ricky was trouble right from the start, muscling his way into the world 10 weeks before anybody expected him, charging feet first.

It was a cold, dark afternoon — the first day of December 1949. Just after lunch, 28-year-old Dorothy Prangley felt a fire flare up low near her stomach as she went about her routine household duties. Dorothy had been through the drill three times before. Three pregnancies. Three babies. She knew what labor was. She knew how labor felt. That's why dread seized her that afternoon as the flame rose and spread and kept her from her chores. Although she tried to deny it, Dorothy was sure this was the real thing. She was in labor, and her baby wasn't due for 2 ½ months.

Dorothy's older boy, a 6-year-old, was in school. The younger children — a girl, 3, and a boy, just over 8 months — were napping. Dorothy's husband, John, was at work. John was a produce manager at a small supermarket not far from the family home in Jenison, a western suburb of Grand Rapids, Michigan's second largest city.

Struggling to keep her rising panic from overwhelming her, Dorothy addressed the emergency systematically. She telephoned John at work and reported the labor pains. Then she called the next-door neighbor, and arranged for her to stay with the kids. Waiting for John, Dorothy told herself over and over again that maybe she *wasn't* in labor. Maybe she was jumping to conclusions. The pain told her otherwise. This was no false alarm. She was in labor, 10 weeks early. Dorothy was scared.

John arrived in his pick-up truck. The short ride to St. Mary's Hospital in Grand Rapids only confirmed Dorothy's fears that both she and her baby were in trouble. Each bump in the road sent a shock of pain through her body. It hadn't been that way with her other children. As she stared out the car windshield at the bleak winter landscape, Dorothy saw rough times ahead. She prayed to God to help her through them.

From St. Mary's Hospital, a nurse called the Prangleys' family doctor, who had monitored the pregnancy. Not that there had been much to monitor. Dorothy's fourth pregnancy had been perfectly normal, just like the previous three. There had been no reason to take any extra precautions. In the examining room, Dorothy was medicated to keep her calm and ease the pain until the doctor could get there. Upon his arrival, he briefly examined Dorothy, then wheeled her into the delivery room.

Out in the waiting room — this was before men were permitted, or inclined, to participate in the birth of their children — John Prangley paced back and forth. From where he stood, the worst was over. He had been through this three times before. He knew, of course, that things were different this time; the baby was well ahead of schedule. But premature babies, as he understood it, were fairly common. They were in good hands — in a modern, well-equipped hospital with competent doctors. Soon the doctor would emerge from the delivery room to report the sex of John's fourth child and tell him that the mother and baby were doing OK.

But in the delivery room, the worst was far from over. Dorothy's legs were fitted into stainless steel stirrups. The anesthesiologist covered her nose and mouth with a mask while a nurse prepared a spinal injection. The baby was upside down, trying to come feet first, and so the contractions, as powerful and painful as they were, weren't doing their job. The baby's arms and legs, his elbows and knees, all acted like hooks, catching on the birth canal. It was like an arrowhead being pulled backward through flesh. In an attempt to turn the baby around, Dr. Morrow used forceps and other instruments, squeezing the baby's fragile, premature skull.

At 4:48 p.m., the torturous journey ended. Weighing exactly three pounds, the baby emerged with the umbilical cord twisted around his neck. The newborn, a boy, entered the world traumatized and, as it would turn out, irrevocably damaged, his first beating behind him. But that revelation belonged to the future. For the moment, the important question was whether the child would live or die. A nurse rushed the child to an incubator, where he received oxygen and heat. Maybe he would live; maybe he wouldn't.

The Prangleys were Roman Catholics. Under normal conditions, their son would have been baptized a month or two after his birth. John and Dorothy would have chosen a godmother and godfather for little Ricky. The godparents would have come to the church for the baptism. And after the session at church, there would have been a buffet lunch at the Prangley home.

But one of the teachings of the church held that a baby who died before being cleansed of its "original sin" — the sin with which every human being is born — would go not to heaven, but to limbo, a region between heaven and hell, where it would remain until judgment day. At the request of the Prangleys, who were reluctant to leave their son's soul in jeopardy, a chaplain at St. Mary's Hospital administered an emergency baptism to Richard Leigh Prangley on Dec. 2, 1949, one day after he was born, clearing the infant's path to heaven.

Ricky lived through the first couple of days, then the first week. For the first three weeks, he received all nourishment through feeding tubes inserted into the veins of his head. For the first three months, Ricky lived, bereft of his parents' touch, beneath the glass bubble of an incubator in a room reserved for critically ill infants. In that sterile room of harsh lighting, chrome and buzzing, blinking machines, the only hands infants felt were the efficient, professional hands of the nurses.

In the first months of Ricky's life, John and Dorothy Prangley were given little opportunity to forge any emotional bonds with their new son. And maybe, they reasoned, it was better that way. After all, the odds were not in Ricky's favor.

But despite his dangerous arrival and his precarious first few months in the world, John and Dorothy Prangley's fourth child slowly gained weight and grew stronger. Right from the start, Ricky was trouble, but Ricky was a survivor.

Three months after his birth, damaged in ways that would become apparent only gradually as the years went by, Ricky went home to the two-story, white wood-framed house at 22 Port Sheldon Street in Jenison.

Like Grand Rapids, Jenison was a stronghold of Dutch Reformed conservatism. Although Grand Rapids was settled by New England Yankees, the city drew its character mainly from the Dutch immigrants who began arriving in western Michigan in the 1870s.

In the 1950s, the residents of the area were largely Republican and mainly believed strongly in free-market economics and cultural conservatism: Survival of the fittest.

While Ricky's grip on life was secure by then, his toehold in his family soon grew tenuous. Even in his early infancy, Dorothy Prangley began to see things in Ricky's behavior that were not right. She described them as "hyperactivity" and "purposeless behavior." His physical development lagged behind, but not excessively so. Ricky was weaned at about one year. Shortly after he turned 1, he was able to sit up by himself, and soon thereafter he stood up and took his first steps. However, he didn't start talking until he was 4, and then only in rudimentary, short phrases, often simply mimicking what somebody else said.

Toilet training came at an average age, but Ricky was plagued by diarrhea. As he grew older and started to eat solid food, Dorothy had to watch her son's diet very closely. Generally he had a bowel movement immediately after every meal. Ricky's naturally loose bowels weren't helped by the fact that he was constantly drinking — milk, juice, water; whatever he could get his hands on. It didn't seem possible that the boy could be that thirsty; more likely it was just another symptom of his restless nature.

But more than the delays — more than the diarrhea and the restlessness and the babyish speech — it was Ricky's curious, inexplicable actions that alarmed his parents. At age 1, for example, he would sit in his high chair, stare at the ceiling and laugh uncontrollably, as though he were possessed. And that was nothing compared with the way he destroyed things, for no particular reason. The stronger he got, the more destruction he caused. He tore open his mattress and smashed the furniture in his bedroom.

Eventually, John and Dorothy were forced to take everything out of their son's room except his bed. There was more. Since birth, Ricky was easily frightened. He was afraid of the dark. He was afraid of heights. And, most of all, he was afraid of suffocating. A piece of clothing that slipped over his face accidentally, or while his mother was dressing him, threw Ricky into a fit of panic.

There seemed to be no end to Ricky's quirks. At age 3, he was able to vomit at will, and seemed to enjoy it. And then there was the food business. Like some kind of animal, Ricky would hold half his dinner in his mouth, then go around the house spitting it out, bit by bit. At about the same age, he began biting himself, leaving teeth marks in his arm and sometimes drawing blood.

From the day Ricky was born, John and Dorothy Prangley were advised of the possibility that their son had emerged from his violent birth with brain damage, but they preferred to believe his outlandish behavior was an emotional problem. As evidence of that, they pointed to the fact that Ricky exhibited greater control in the presence of his father — the designated disciplinarian of the family. If it was a physical problem — if his self-control circuit had been wiped out during his birth — then how could he turn it on at all?

The emotional-origin theory was easier to accept because it was more fixable. Maybe maturity would help. Maybe all that bizarre behavior was just a long phase that Ricky would outgrow. If only John and Dorothy could get their son to be more in control of himself. If only they could get him to behave! John tried all the usual disciplinary techniques, graduating from scoldings, to spankings, to enforced isolation.

When Ricky was good, he could sleep in the same room with his brothers. When he wasn't, he slept alone, in a room he came to know as the "punishment room." Sometimes John Prangley used sheets to restrain his son in his bed in the punishment room at night. It was for his own safety. A natural night owl, Ricky had gotten into the habit of wandering around the house late into the night.

He especially liked to stand by an open window in the summer and listen to the crickets chirp. If Ricky had been a normal child, his parents might have been able to tolerate his nocturnal wanderings. But who knew what mischief a boy like Ricky could create if allowed to roam the house at night? So John Prangley restrained Ricky in his bed.

The punishment room didn't help. In fact, nothing that John Prangley tried seemed to make an impression on his son. Throughout Ricky's early childhood, the wild behavior continued. Ricky's capacity to cause chaos was boundless. He didn't sit down; he hurled himself into a chair. He didn't walk from one room to another; he charged. He moved at a gallop; he spoke in a roar. He urinated into the heat registers, he lifted up the floor grates and dropped toys, or books, or his father's shoes, into the ductwork. He saw the glow from the furnace and imagined a great fire burning deep beneath the floorboards and thought that he was feeding it. More toys, he thought, would produce more heat. Ricky plugged up keyholes with pencil erasers. He stuck bobby pins into electrical sockets. He once filled the bathtub with water and gave his parents' collection of 33 r.p.m. records a bath. It was an act that would earn him a spanking he never would forget.

When Ricky was 4, his parents began taking him to doctors, mainly to help correct his speech, which fell further and further behind. That's when the Prangleys first started hearing the phrase "organic brain damage" used as a diagnosis, rather than as a speculation. Reluctantly, John and Dorothy began to accept the possibility that Ricky's problems *were* organic. None of the other possibilities seemed to fit.

The Prangleys had tried every kind of discipline available to reasonable, loving parents. Their prayers hadn't helped. Time hadn't helped, either. Maturity did nothing to calm Ricky down. It simply made him bigger and louder and stronger, increasing his power to upset the tranquility of his home. He couldn't function at all in school. His attempts to socialize with other kids in the neighborhood always ended in fights. He spent more and more nights sleeping in the punishment room.

John and Dorothy Prangley were caring, responsible parents. They did what parents of their era were supposed to do. John got up and went to work each day so that he could give his children everything they needed. Dorothy kept a clean, efficient house and looked after the children. The Prangleys knew that rearing children wasn't supposed to be a picnic. They were prepared for the normal struggles and sacrifices. They didn't expect perfect children. They expected a reasonable amount of rambunctiousness from their kids. But Ricky was something else entirely. Ricky was a challenge for which they weren't prepared. Ricky wasn't just a difficult child, he was a disturbance to his family, constantly upsetting the natural peace and order of the household.

By the time Ricky turned 6, three more Prangley children had been born. There were seven then. Eventually, there would be 11. And Ricky was a bigger handful than all the others combined. Sure, Ricky was as much a part of the family as any of the other six children, but it wasn't fair to the other kids to be forced to live with such a disruptive influence. How could John and Dorothy give the other kids the attention they needed when they couldn't let Ricky out of their sight? How could the Prangleys ever be a normal, happy family as long as Ricky was causing trouble every step of the way?

Like every parent of a child whose handicap becomes evident in stages, John and Dorothy Prangley gradually arrived at the realization that Ricky was not — and probably never would be — a normal child.

Day by day, the evidence mounted. In the beginning, the Prangleys prayed for a miracle cure — an operation, maybe, or a prescription — that would fix the problem. Further along, they prayed for divine intervention. After all, God wasn't limited by the restrictions of medicine. God could fix anything. When God didn't fix Ricky, the Prangleys began searching for a more earthly solution. Ultimately, they stopped looking for a cure; they started looking for relief. They owed it to their other children.

John and Dorothy Prangley weren't ones to seek outside help with their personal problems. John, especially, took pride in the fact that he always had been able to take care of himself and his family on his own. He was always able to find his own solutions to his troubles. But then, John Prangley never counted on a Ricky in his life.

Maybe he just didn't have the right tools; maybe this was a case for the experts. The Prangleys began seeking advice and gathering information. They spoke to Ricky's doctors, their family doctor, their priest. They heard that there were, indeed, places for children like Ricky.

The Departure

I remember my father talking to me in the car — telling me I was going to a new home. I couldn't understand what he meant by that. I didn't know what he meant. I don't remember feeling scared. I remember feeling confused. I just didn't understand.

— Richard Prangley

In December 1955, Ricky turned 6, and by then John and Dorothy Prangley were sure there would be no quick fix. They conceded, in fact, that there probably would be no fix at all. But maybe improvement was possible.

Maybe, the Prangleys theorized, they just hadn't figured out the right approach. Maybe Ricky needed more regimentation in his life. There was a chance, they thought, that institutional life — for a short period, anyway — would finally instill in Ricky the self-control that had eluded him until that point in his life. One of the possibilities was the Coldwater State Home and Training School in the town of Coldwater, about 100 miles southeast of the town where the Prangleys lived. Maybe it wouldn't hurt Ricky to go there for a little while. Maybe he would come home a different boy.

But the Prangleys couldn't just drop Ricky off there. It wasn't a summer camp. There were certain procedures that had to be followed.

For one thing, the Prangleys had to acknowledge, for the record, that Ricky was a damaged child. In early January 1956, John Prangley petitioned the Kent County Probate Court to rule that Ricky was mentally handicapped and that an institution was the best place for him. Psychiatric and psychological reports accompanied John Prangley's petition. As for John's personal assessment as to why his son should be committed to Coldwater, here's what he wrote:

He was a 2 ½-month prematurely born child. He was delivered by instruments. He has a brain injury. Child Guidance Clinic advised commitment. He is unable to go to school. He is a slow learner. Has laughter fits. He has a mental age of 4. He becomes excited when strangers come to the house. He is given pills to calm him

7

down. Gets up in the middle of the night and roams around. He tears all his toys apart. He throws paper and other things down hot-air registers.

The doctors claim he has no knowledge of right and wrong. The corporal punishment had no effect upon him. He is not understandable when speaking. He repeats questions rather than giving answers. He can't give his age, nor identify colors. He has temper tantrums and becomes angry. He is afraid of heights. He doesn't play well with other children in the family. The brothers and sisters are becoming aware of Ricky's handicap. The mother is becoming highly nervous because she has to constantly watch Ricky. He wanders away from home when left alone.

He is obedient to father through compulsion, but not to mother. The social worker at the Child Guidance Clinic is quite familiar with this case. He has been seen by a psychiatrist and a psychologist at the Child Guidance Clinic.

At the Child Guidance Clinic of Grand Rapids, Ricky had been examined twice in late January 1956, presumably with the intention of making the case for his commitment to Coldwater. Ricky had been referred to the clinic by the Prangleys' parish priest.

The formal argument for the commitment of Ricky — who suddenly had become "Richard" in the blizzard of paperwork that preceded his commitment to Coldwater — included two identical Kent County Probate Court affidavits in which two doctors, acting under the direction of the court, filled in the blanks and added their comments.

The first doctor, a Grand Rapids doctor who had practiced medicine for nine years, examined Richard Leigh Prangley on Jan. 27, 1956. The doctor judged that Ricky was, "a mentally handicapped person and his condition is such as to require care and treatment in an institution for the care, custody and treatment of such mentally diseased persons and that the facts and circumstances upon which such opinion is based, are as follows: ..."

The doctor's only direct contribution to that statement were the words "mentally handicapped" and "his" (as opposed to "her"). The rest of it was already printed on the form. It was a standard affidavit. In his own handwriting, the doctor added: "His span of attention is short. He wanders about the office, shifting his attention rapidly from one object to another. He speaks few words, mainly the names of objects, but does not speak complete thoughts. He cannot follow simple directions, such as to open a certain door to return to his father in the reception room. He is mentally handicapped due to partial destruction of nervous tissue in the brain."

The second doctor was a graduate of the University of Michigan Medical School and had practiced for 10 years. This doctor examined Ricky on Jan. 23, 1956. He used the words "mentally retarded" to describe Ricky. He filled in the blanks, as the first doctor had done, then added in his own handwriting: "He had a retarded development since birth. Is unmanageable at home. Doesn't know his last name or age. Cannot learn."

On Feb. 7, Kent County Probate Court Judge John Dalton made it official. Based on the testimony of John and Dorothy Prangley, plus the affidavits of the two doctors, Judge Dalton ruled that Ricky was "mentally handicapped" and that he should be admitted to the Coldwater home. He ordered the Prangleys to pay Coldwater $20 per month for "the maintenance of the patient."

But it wasn't quite that simple. Coldwater had a waiting list in those days — particularly for the "custodial care" cases, the kids who had been written off as uneducable and untrainable. On the day after he ordered Ricky into the institution, Judge Dalton wrote to Dr. E. J. Rennell, the medical superintendent there: "This patient [Richard] is one out of a family of seven children. His mother finds it increasingly difficult to continue with her household duties and to continue the care of the patient. His father also strongly urged his admission at this time if possible."

But Superintendant Rennell had a stack of such appeals — most of them urgent. He wrote back to Judge Dalton:

> From the information contained in the commitment papers, it is our opinion that Richard will require a custodial type of care. ["Custodial" was the term used to describe the care of the most severely disabled residents — those who needed round-the-clock care]. Our facilities for this type of case have for a long time been filled to capacity and we have developed a large waiting list. … We can admit a case only as a vacancy occurs. Vacancies are unpredictable and are brought about only by one of two methods:
>   1. Death of patient of this type in the institution.
>   2. Removal of a patient of this type for care at home by relatives (this is a rare occurrence).
>
> Based on the information contained in your letter, we are designating this an emergency case to be given consideration … over less urgent cases … I am sorry to state that even this procedure will not insure an admission in the near future since we have a number of emergency cases who were previously committed and must be given prior consideration for admission."

A true bureaucrat, Rennell couldn't resist the opportunity to take a poke at the Michigan legislature. He added: "This is due … to the failure of the State of Michigan in the past to provide adequate facilities for its mentally handicapped."

The wait, however, wasn't as long as Rennell predicted. On May 25, 1956 — just 3 ½ months after the probate court ruling — John and Dorothy Prangley received a letter from Rennell informing them that they could deliver Ricky to Coldwater anytime within the following 20 days. Meanwhile, Coldwater had requested information from the Child Guidance Center, and in late March 1956, Ricky's social worker wrote to R. G. Mulchahey, director of the Social Services Department at Coldwater:

> Re: Richard Leigh Prangley. In response to your recent request for a summary of our contacts on the above named child, I am enclosing a summary of our material.
>
> As you will note from the material, Richard presents a management problem in regard to his behavior, but we do feel that he would profit from a training program. Therefore, we are recommending him as a candidate for the Training School. We will welcome a report from you as to when the child can be accepted.
>
> If we can be of any further help to you, do not hesitate to make such request.

The summary the Family Guidance Clinic sent to Coldwater went into much further detail than the affidavits of the psychiatrists, beginning with the letter from the Prangley's priest, which, according to the report, "cited a pattern of highly impulsive and uncontrolled behavior, which made Richard a disturbance in the family and an extremely difficult child for his parents to manage."

After detailing all of Ricky's problems, the report to Coldwater summarized the cause of them this way: "It appears to be an almost pure culture brain syndrome, with direct organic behavioral symptoms.... The Coldwater institution, which would be the only facility for him at this time, was suggested to [the parents]. Apparently they could accept the importance of making a special plan for him on the basis of the child's very real damaging influence to the many other children in the family, as well as the real physical drain the child represents to the mother."

A month later, at the request of Coldwater's medical superintendent, John Prangley filled out a 10-page form called a "History Blank," in which he was asked for the reason for requesting admittance of his son to the institution. He wrote:

> For a period during the past two years we had been taking Richard to doctors to receive help — mainly to correct his speech. From the examinations of the doctors, we concede the fact that he received a brain injury at the time of birth. His behavior is bad, mainly because he doesn't realize right from wrong. He's very hard to control, especially by his mother. He must have custodial care at all times. Doesn't seem to be able to concentrate for any length of time at any one thing. He does most things for himself — dresses himself, good toilet manners, eats well. He can't play too long with the other children. Temper tantrums are existing. We feel he could be helped some with special training. If so, we feel it's no more than right to ask him to be committed. Although he might have to be classified as custodial, I believe education might be helpful. We do pray for some help for him.

Later in the questionnaire, when asked to describe his son's personality, John Prangley wrote:

> Richard is a good boy, but just doesn't seem to know right from wrong. I don't think he's capable of showing too much interest in people, being unable to express his wishes. He hasn't changed much in the past two years. He seems to be quite nervous — due mostly to his fear of heights and fear of being spanked when naughty. He's very friendly, though — really gets too excited if company arrives. Seems to employ too much energy.
>
> Sure hope he will be able to receive some training toward these respects.

Ricky, of course, never realized that a judge had ruled that he was mentally defective. He didn't know that a case was being made for his commitment to Coldwater. He didn't know that his name had been placed on a waiting list.

Ricky remained oblivious to his parents' plan until the morning of June 4, when, following one more night for Ricky in the punishment room, John Prangley came into the room and started packing Ricky's clothes into a suitcase. *All* of them.

John Prangley told his son that he would be going for a long ride in the car. Ricky was all for it. He loved car rides, particularly long ones. He found the peaceful hum of the engine and the steady motion soothing. It was one of the few places Ricky could sit still for more than a minute or two. After breakfast, Ricky jumped into the back seat of the family station wagon while his father slid behind the wheel. Dorothy sat beside him in the front seat. It was a warm, overcast day on the brink of summer.

After all those trips to clinics in recent months, it didn't seem odd to Ricky that none of his siblings was going along for the ride. He assumed he and his parents simply were going to see another one of those people who asked so many questions. It was, indeed, a long ride, just as John Prangley promised. Ricky sat by a window in the spacious second seat of the three-seat wagon and watched the road signs and farm fields pass by.

Then, about halfway into the trip, something unsettling happened. Suddenly John Prangley started talking about Ricky's "new home."

New home? What was that supposed to mean? Was the Prangley family moving from their house on Port Sheldon Street? Was that what his father was trying to say? No, that wasn't it. Only Ricky was moving. In his new home, John Prangley said, Ricky would learn the discipline and self-control that would allow him to return to his real home, with his real family.

It was too much for any 6-year-old to grasp. Ricky had no way of knowing at that moment that his life was about to undergo a cataclysmic change. Leaning over the back of the front seat, the only question he could think of was when he could go back to his real home.

"Someday," his father said.

Eventually, John Prangley steered the station wagon onto a long, winding driveway. Ricky saw a massive red brick building with steel bars on the windows. As he climbed out of the car, he felt confused. This was the new home his father had been talking about? It didn't look anything like a home to Ricky. He kept hoping he had misunderstood the "new home" business. Maybe he was there, after all, to see another doctor, a speculation supported by the appearance of an attendant in a white coat who met the Prangleys inside the administration building, where John and Dorothy answered questions and signed papers.

About 2 p.m., with no further explanation, John and Dorothy Prangley got up from their chairs. Dorothy embraced her son, then turned quickly and walked out of the office. John told his son to be a good boy and to do what the attendants told him to do. Then, never looking back, the Prangleys climbed into their car and drove back to Jenison. Ricky was not allowed to watch the car disappear.

A white-uniformed attendant led the bewildered boy from the administration building to another building. They walked down a hallway to a large steel door with a square window, into a large, sparsely furnished room where 40 or 50 boys loitered on wooden benches that were bolted together and pushed against white brick walls.

These weren't the kind of boys Ricky knew from his neighborhood. They were different somehow. Some of them sprawled on the floor. Some of them wore strange jackets that didn't allow them to move their arms. One boy was hitting himself. One was repeatedly slamming himself onto the floor.

The whole frightening scene rose from an overwhelming stench of human feces and urine.

This was one of the dayrooms of Cottage 41, which provided shelter to about 250 kids designated for "custodial care." These were boys with no prospects. Uneducable. Untrainable. In some cases, unmanageable.

Cottage 41 included four wards, one for each of three different age categories, plus a fourth ward for the lowest of the "low-grades" — the most severely disabled residents. Because Ricky was toilet trained and could feed himself, he escaped the very bottom rung. He was one rung up. Each ward consisted of a dayroom and a barracks-like dormitory. The wards shared a common dining room. Cottage 41 provided food and shelter and almost nothing else — nothing good, anyway.

Ricky looked around at his unfathomable surroundings and wondered how soon it would be before his parents came to take him back home. In fact, he would never go home again. Not even for a weekend or holiday.

Or, as the staff kept telling him in his early days at Coldwater, this *was* his home.

On that day in early June, when most 6-year-old boys were anticipating the freedom of summer recess, Richard Prangley, No. 4279, was starting a 15-year prison sentence. Of course he didn't know it. In fact, he had no clue as to what was happening to him. As far as he knew, he still lived in the white house with his big family. As far as he knew, he was still just Ricky.

Cottage 41

At first, I waited every day for my parents to come and get me. Boy, I hated that place. I kept asking the attendants, "When am I going home? When am I going home?" They said, "You are home — you might as well get used to it."

— Richard Prangley

In the late 1860s, the City of Coldwater's representative in the Michigan Senate, C. D. Randall, drafted legislation to create a state-supported school for orphaned and dependent children. His intention was to replace the hodgepodge of poorhouses and orphanages that had developed over the years.

A reformer, Randall thought the orphanages were inadequate warehouses where children were stored and fed like cattle. The state, Randall felt, should do better. After Randall's bill passed in 1872, the state advertised it was accepting bids. Sixteen cities responded. The city of Coldwater, offering 20 acres of land, plus $25,000 toward construction of the school, edged out the city of Jackson.

The original facility — one main building and eight residential "cottages" — was built at a cost of $425,000. In May 1874, the school opened its doors to 150 children. They were 4–16 years old, healthy and of sound mind. Thus Michigan became the first state in the union to provide a home and school for neglected and dependent children. In fact, the school was the first institution of its kind in the world to be funded by public money. Michigan was honored for that distinction at the Paris Exposition in the late 1800s.

The main building at Coldwater State Home included classrooms and a dining area for all residents. The cottages were behind the main building. Each cottage was designed for 25 residents and included live-in facilities for staff members. They were specifically designed to be small, reflecting the belief of the time that an intimate, homelike atmosphere was essential for preparing the children for reentry into the community. There was also a chapel on the grounds.

Almost from the beginning, there was an attempt to open the school to kids with physical or mental disabilities or illnesses. Some even made it through the doors, but once their handicaps were discovered they were returned to the counties from which they came.

The school was highly regimented. The children wore uniforms; members of the staff were stern disciplinarians. A punishment report dated Nov. 10, 1876 records: "Charles was sent to bed for one day and fed bread and water for stealing a ball from Eugene. I have tried repeatedly to correct his pilfering habits by talking to him, but without much success and I thought I would give him an opportunity to reflect a little."

The principal goal of the school was to place children back into the world at large, and it enjoyed considerable success. By June 1932, 455 children lived in the facility, 900 were in homes under supervision of the school and 3,601 had been legally adopted.

In 1935, the school yielded to pressures to use the school for children other than orphans and dependent children. Renamed the Michigan Children's Village, the school opened its doors to mildly-to-moderately retarded children. In 1939, the agency changed its name to Coldwater State Home and Training School and began admitting residents of all levels of development — physically and mentally. The population of the school soared, forcing a seemingly endless series of new buildings and expansion projects.

In that first year under the new name, 10 cottages capable of housing nearly 1,200 residents were built. Still, it wasn't enough. In 1949, the year Richard Prangley was born, buildings 41 and 42 were completed, each designed for 224 residents. In 1952, the expansion exploded. It included two residential buildings for about 100 residents in need of treatment for severe behavior problems; an infirmary for 80 residents; and the largest residential building of all, for 300 babies and toddlers.

In 1956, a 100-bed hospital was completed and, in 1957, the last two residential structures were built. Each had room for 224 residents.

Only later, after this monstrosity of a complex had been created, did the pendulum swing the other way — toward smaller, more humane settings. Eventually the deinstitutionalization movement would close the place entirely as a facility for the developmentally disabled.

In the mid-1980s, the Michigan Department of Corrections would take over the Coldwater grounds, creating two medium-security prisons — the Florence Crane Women's Facility and the Lakeland Correctional Facility for men. In 1995, Camp Branch, a women's minimum-security lockup, would be added to the mix. But all of that was a long way off in the spring of 1956.

When Richard Prangley arrived at the institutional-red brick complex called the Coldwater State Home and Training School, its sprawl was at its zenith. There were 27 buildings in all. The boys were housed on one side of the complex; the girls on the other.

On that afternoon in early June when Richard first walked into the day-room of Cottage 41, he weighed 49 pounds and was 47 inches tall. He brought with him one brown jacket, three T-shirts, two undershirts, four pairs of shorts, nine shirts, two pairs of pajamas, one wool sweater, 12 colored T-shirts, two pairs of blue jeans, one pair of brown dress pants, one pair of overalls, one pair of cow-boy pants, one pair of brown oxfords, seven pairs of socks and $2 in cash.

After spending a few hours in the nightmarish dayroom of Cottage 41, Ward II, Richard had dinner. Then, lonely, scared, confused and wondering why his parents had left him in that place, Richard put his head under his blanket and cried himself to sleep.

The first week seemed like a month to Richard. Day after day, hour after hour, he sat on the wooden benches in the dayroom, where the residents were left to pass the hours as best they could. Richard cried until he didn't have any tears left, waiting for his parents to come and take him home, wondering how they could have forgotten him.

During that same week, an attendant had a different perspective on Richard's adjustment, as recorded on a form called "Attitude of Patient":

> Sunday: Richard has made a good adjustment.
> Monday: Admitted to hospital.
> Tuesday: Apparently not homesick yet; eats good.
> Wednesday: Eats and sleeps well; a little homesick today.
> Thursday: He is a tidy patient.
> Friday: Eats and sleeps well; gets along good with other patients.
> Saturday: A pleasant patient; seems happy.

About six weeks after he arrived at Coldwater, Richard received his first of the half-dozen or so psychological evaluations he would get in the coming years.

> OBSERVATIONS: Richard is a neat, good-looking boy, who, from outward appearances, seems to be more alert than he actually is. He seemed to have a poor understanding of the test situation and approached it as though it were a game, revealing a short attention span and poor concentration. He attempted a response to every item, apparently giving no thought to the possibility of failure. His speech is infantile and poorly developed, making it difficult to understand him and causing frequent repetitions.
>
> Richard established a basal age at the 2 ½-year level and his successes extended through year 3 ½. His vocabulary is limited and most of his failures occurred on problems requiring the knowledge of a variety of words. Language comprehension was good, however, and he was able to follow directions well. His ability in the performance field was only fair and he displayed a very short attention span.

The results of the evaluation:

> Chronological Age: 6 years, 7 months.
> Mental Age: 3 years.
> Intelligence Quotient: 46.
> Classification: High-grade Imbecile.

Noting that Richard had scored 69 on the Merrill-Palmer Scale when tested at the Grand Rapids Child Guidance Clinic the previous March, the evaluator wrote: "Since Richard appeared to cooperate well, and there is nothing of significance in his test pattern, no reason can be offered for the wide discrepancy between previous and present test results. He has made a slow adjustment to his cottage and those who care for him do not consider him to be particularly alert. However, the boy may have been homesick at the time of this test and probably should be re-tested in order to compare results."

Homesick? Richard was completely disoriented. Worse than that, he was devastated. And why wouldn't he be? One day he was part of a family, living in a snug house with loving parents and brothers and sisters. The next day, he was living in a human warehouse with hundreds of volatile strangers supervised by attendants, most of whose attitudes ranged from indifference to contempt.

Every day was the same. After breakfast, Richard and the other residents deemed to be uneducable and untrainable were released into the dayroom of Cottage 41, Ward II, where they would spend an aimless, unstructured day, watching the hours drip away, one by one, like water from a leaky faucet. Richard spent most of his day daydreaming about his *real* home, wondering where his parents were and when they were going to come and take him away from that place.

One month after Richard arrived at Coldwater — eight days before that first psychological evaluation — John and Dorothy Prangley returned to the institution. Dorothy hugged and kissed her son. John shook Richard's hand and led him to the station wagon.

The moment Richard saw his parents, he started squirming like an excited puppy. When he climbed into the car with his parents and his father started the car's engine, Richard didn't give a second thought to his belongings back in the dorm of Cottage 41. He didn't care if ever saw them again. The important thing was that he was leaving this horrible place. Finally, he was going home.

Then another confusing thing happened. Just a few minutes after John Prangley steered the station wagon off the Coldwater grounds, he pulled into the parking lot of a restaurant in town. Richard would have preferred to go straight home — to put as many miles between him and the Cottage 41 dayroom as possible, as quickly as possible. But that was OK; he enjoyed a restaurant meal as much as any kid. He had waited a month to go home; one more hour wouldn't make much difference.

What started out as a joyous occasion quickly became tense and awkward as John and Dorothy Prangley continued to sidestep Richard's comments about how glad he was to be going home. They kept shifting the conversation back to how things were going at *the* home — Richard's *new* home.

Richard told them in no uncertain terms that he didn't like it. He tried to describe the stench of the dayroom and the cruel unpredictability of the other residents. They'd be playing tag or chasing after a ball together, and suddenly they'd start punching or kicking the nearest child. Richard showed his parents his lumps and bruises. John and Dorothy admonished their son for exaggerating. They told him it couldn't be that bad. They encouraged him to try harder to get along.

When the meal was over, another terrible and baffling thing occurred: Richard's father pointed the station wagon back toward the Coldwater home and Cottage 41. Again, Richard's parents left him there. Before they drove away, Richard asked when they would be coming back to take him home. John Prangley gave his standard reply:

"Someday."

In his first weeks at Coldwater, Richard asked the question every day — sometimes every hour of every day. It was the only question that mattered to him: When would he be going home? The attendants were more honest than Richard's father. They told him, over and over again, that he *was* home and that he might as well get used to it. But Richard kept telling himself that it couldn't be true. This was *not* his home. He could never get used to it.

On Nov. 30, the day before Richard turned 7, John Prangley came back to Coldwater with Richard's grandmother. The three went out for a birthday dinner. Again Richard dared to hope for the best birthday gift of all — a return home — and again he heard that hateful answer: He *was* home.

John Prangley and his mother-in-law returned to Jenison. Richard went back to Cottage 41.

One month after he turned 7, Richard was reevaluated by the same Coldwater psychologist who did the first evaluation. It was a crucial event in Richard's life. The purpose of the evaluation was to determine whether Richard was capable of moving to a cottage for the "trainable," or if he should remain in the "custodial" cottage, where he would be merely stored.

If the psychologist had determined at that point that Richard was capable of learning, he would have been sent to one of the "line cottages" — so named because they stood in a line stretching out from the administration building. The boys in the line cottages — particularly the young boys — received vocational, and even academic, training. A move to one of the line cottages would have put Richard's life on an entirely different course.

That didn't happen.

If the conclusions drawn from the first test didn't seal his fate, the results of the second one surely did.

> OBSERVATIONS: Richard is a small boy who is rather infantile in his reactions to new people and situations. However, at this time, he approached the test in a more interested way than he did during the admission examination and appeared to put forth good effort for a child his age. His speech is poorly developed and consists primarily of single words and short phrases. He rarely verbalizes a complete thought without intermittent questions. Richard is a distractible child, but was easily controlled with praise and encouragement.
>
> Richard established a basal age at the 3-year level and his success extended through year 5. His earliest and most consistent failures occurred on problems measuring range of vocabulary and verbal expression. Comprehension for both verbally and pictorially presented material was also poor. His highest successes included performance and simple memory items.

The examination showed Richard's chronological age as 7 years, 1 month; his mental age as 3 years, 11 months. He had an intelligence quotient (IQ) of 55, and he was classified as a "low-grade moron." According to the summary:

> At the time of his previous test, it was the opinion of the examiner that Richard was not functioning as high as possible, probably due to homesickness. Present results probably give a better indication as to his actual ability. Although these results indicate that Richard should be capable of adjusting satisfactorily to a trainable group, he is so extremely infantile in his behavior that it is feared that the sudden change may have a detrimental effect, socially. It is felt that if a change is made gradually, he may adapt more easily. For example, if he is transferred first to cottage 21, and then to a "trainable" cottage, he will not feel the competition so keenly. He is definitely trainable and should eventually be considered for academic training.

For reasons that aren't clear from Richard's records, that transition never happened. Except for brief, sporadic stays in the "higher-grade" cottages, that final recommendation never came to fruition. Richard would remain in Cottage 41, custodial care, for the next 12 years, a period that took him, in chronological terms anyway, from childhood to adulthood.

For 11 years, beginning in 1962, Edward Gifford was an admissions social worker at the Coldwater State Home. In 1997, he was an adult services worker for the Department of Social Services in Ingham County.

When Gifford went to work at Coldwater, there were 3,000 residents in the institution and 500 more waiting to get in. Gifford's job was to investigate the situations of those on the waiting list and prioritize them. Although Gifford apparently never crossed paths with Richard while they were both at Coldwater, he closely followed Richard's story after 1980, when the state media began publishing and broadcasting stories about the man who was locked away in a horrible place called the Coldwater State Home and Training School.

Gifford had two reasons to feel defensive about those reports. Not only had he been a member of the institution's staff for 11 years, he grew up in the town of Coldwater, where his father was a dentist. Part of growing up in Coldwater, the town, was getting used to out-of-town criticism of the institution.

What did the out-of-towners know? The citizens of Coldwater were intimately acquainted with the people who worked inside the institution. They were friends and relatives and neighbors. They were good, honest, hard-working people. Every time the press portrayed the state home as a den of mismanagement and abuse — which was mostly the way the press portrayed it — the whole town looked bad. Reading the stories about Richard, Gifford couldn't help but feel that they were one-sided. The stories all made it sound as if the institution were some kind of a snake pit when, in fact, it served a real purpose.

For one thing, it was an important option for people unable to cope at home with their severely disabled children. The fact is that some kids were, because of their disabilities, too much for untrained people to handle — even if they were sincere, caring people who wanted the best for their children. Second, most of the kids at Coldwater, according to Gifford, *did* receive academic and vocational training at schools that rivaled those in the public school system. In fact, it was only the kids in custodial care — the hopeless causes — who spent their time loitering in the dayrooms. For the most part, Gifford said, these were the kind of kids who crawled around on the floor and had no control over their bodily functions. What else could a civilized society do with people like this?

In another era, their disabilities probably would have killed them at birth, or shortly thereafter. Modern medicine kept them alive and left them on society's doorstep. Surely a caring society must feed and house them and make them as comfortable as possible. But why waste everybody's time pretending they could learn something, or that one day they would contribute to society? The institution spelled out its approach in an undated brochure called a "Circular of Information":

> The Coldwater State Home and Training School is an institution for the care, supervision, education and training of mentally retarded (feeble-minded) persons. The patients' age, size, physical condition, level of mental development, habits and behavior are important factors influencing the type of training for which the patient is eligible. There are also restrictions imposed by the facilities which the institution has to offer.

Academic education is offered only to those who fall within the proper age limits, and who can meet the necessary intellectual requirements. Vocational training is given those able to participate and to benefit. For those unfortunate individuals whose intellectual ability is extremely limited, the institution can offer only care, supervision and a minimum of habit training.

For whatever reason, Richard Prangley was deemed to be one those "unfortunate individuals."

This, Gifford said, was the part of Richard's story that always baffled him. He couldn't imagine why Richard was put in Cottage 41 in the first place and why he was left to languish there for so long. According to Gifford, there was a continuous review process in place. He could see how the initial mistake was made. Obviously, Richard's placement was based on the conclusions of the two psychologists who evaluated him before he arrived at the institution. But why was that mistake allowed to stand? Surely somebody would have noticed that Richard was capable of learning.

On the other hand, maybe it wasn't as baffling as it seemed. The pecking order at Coldwater was largely a matter of IQ. As Gifford recalled it, the magic number was 50. Kids who tested above 50 almost always went to cottages for the "educable" or "trainable." For those who fell below 50, anything could happen. An average IQ is considered to be 100.

In Richard's case, it was important to remember that he arrived at Coldwater with at least two strikes against him — the evaluations of the two psychologists whose affidavits became part of the case for his commitment. One of them said flatly that Richard was incapable of learning. On his first test at Coldwater, administered just one month after he arrived there, Richard scored 46 on the Revised Stanford-Binet Scale. That's when he was labeled a "High-grade Imbecile."

How accurate were these tests in measuring a person's potential? If Richard's case is any indication, they were an absolute travesty. His roller-coaster ride on the IQ scale went like this:

In March 1956, at the Grand Rapids Child Guidance Clinic, Richard's IQ was measured as 69 on the Merrill-Palmer Scale, making him, in the words of the psychologist who tested him "brain-damaged."

In July 1956, as noted above, his IQ was 46, according to the Revised Stanford-Binet Scale, making him a "high-grade imbecile." He was 6 years, 7 months; his "mental age" was said to be 3 years.

In Dec. 1956, his IQ was 55, as measured by Stanford-Binet and he was promoted from "high-grade imbecile" to "low-grade moron." He was 7 years, 1 month; mentally, the test supposedly said, he was 3 years, 11 months.

If Richard was tested between 1956 and 1964, there is no record of it. Here's how the rest of the tests went:

In March 1964, when Richard was 14, he was again classified as a "high-grade imbecile" according to something called the Vineland Social Maturity Scale. This pegged Richard's "developmental age" at 6 years, 11 months.

In March 1968, when he was 18, his IQ measured 39 on Stanford-Binet, but by then that was considered "moderate retardation." His "mental age" was said to be 6 years, 8 months.

But then some kind of miracle happened. Nine months later, Richard achieved a Full Scale IQ of 70 on the Wechsler Adult Intelligence Scale, which earned him a "borderline" designation.

An astonishing metamorphosis? Unlikely. A more logical explanation is that the tests were worthless in defining Richard Prangley. Ultimately, even the most optimistic assessments of Richard's potential would fall far short of reality.

Invalid though they were, the early tests doomed Richard to a wasted youth. Excerpts from Form 2000, a daily-activity report in Richard's records from Coldwater, sketches the hollow life to which the early tests doomed him, all too easily compressing 15 years into 11 pages. Some typical entries:

1. June 4, 1956: RECEIVED at the Coldwater State Home and Training School by probate court commitment of Kent County. Brought from home by parents, Mr. and Mrs. John Prangley, 22 Port Sheldon, Grandville, Mich. Taken to hospital admission. Operative permission blank signed by father and filed in record.
2. June 4, 1956: TRANSFERRED to Cottage 41, first assignment.
3. June 15, 1956: INJURY: Richard fell against a bench; sustained a laceration in the middle of his forehead. Form "A." [The attendants filled out Form "A," also know as an "Incident Report," to document disruptive or antisocial behavior.]
4. July 5, 1956: INTERVIEW: The parents were in the office regarding his progress and they were told that he had not yet had a psychometric examination and while he appeared to be happy and he was adjusting satisfactorily, we could not give them much information regarding him at this time.
5. Aug. 10, 1956: HOSPITAL: Admitted with gastroenteritis and diarrhea. Placed on Kaopectate and neomycin.
6. Oct. 24, 1956: INJURY: Richard was found to have a black eye (right). Cause unknown. Form "A."
7. Nov. 30, 1956: INTERVIEW: Father of this patient in the office to inquire as to the progress of his son. He apparently feels that the boy has considerable more ability than has been demonstrated by the test results and asked that a reevaluation of the boy be done so that when he stops in at the office at some future date we may be able to give him further information as to the boy's possible potentials.

Each of these reports ends with a note identifying the medication Richard was receiving at the time. In 1958, two years after he arrived at Coldwater,

Richard started receiving tranquilizers — first compazine, then thorazine, the drug viewed in those days as the silver bullet for hyperactivity.

In July 1958, when Richard was 9 ½ years old and weighed 70 pounds, he was receiving 200 milligrams of thorazine, which caused a dramatic decrease in his reports of bad behavior. It was no wonder — on 200 milligrams of thorazine, Richard could hardly stay awake. Often after receiving his lunch-time dose, he'd fall asleep on the hard wooden benches in the dayroom, dozing summer afternoons away while the other kids played kickball outside.

This was a source of great unhappiness for Richard. Outside recreation was the only thing he enjoyed in those days, and to awaken late in the afternoon, hot and dazed from a drug-induced sleep, only to find that he had missed it again was always a crushing disappointment.

As soon as he was old enough to make the connection between the pills the attendants made him swallow and the lethargy that seized him after lunch, Richard tried to refuse the pills, in which case the attendants would literally shove them down his throat. Once Richard got the hang of deception, he'd pretend to swallow the pills, hide them under his tongue, then toss them under the lunch table as soon as the attendants turned their backs.

In early 1967, after being transferred to Cottage 42 and a training program, he stopped receiving the tranquilizers altogether.

As for Richard's health, letters from the physicians at Coldwater to John and Dorothy Prangley describe an assortment of routine maladies:

1. Jan. 14, 1958: Dear Mr. and Mrs. Prangley: We wish to advise you that Richard had his tonsils and adenoids removed this morning. Richard is recovering nicely from the operation and he is resting comfortably at this time. We do not anticipate any complications but if any occur, we will notify you.
2. March 29, 1967: Dear Mr. and Mrs. Prangley: We wish to advise you that your son, Richard Leigh Prangley, underwent foot surgery today at the institution hospital, to correct chronic infected nails on both great toes.
3. March 13, 1969: Dear Mr. and Mrs. Prangley: Laboratory tests on your son … reveal that he does have infectious hepatitis. At present he is doing fine and we do not anticipate any difficulties.

The periodic "Unusual Incident Report" forms and "Patient Accident and Behavior Report" forms in Richard's file tell a little more:

1. Oct. 4, 1960, 5 a.m., Cottage 41: While in the stool room [another resident] and Richard Prangley had a fight over toilet tissue. Before I could separate them, Richard received two marks on his upper lip; appear to be finger nail marks.

2. May 5, 1962, 7:30 p.m., Cottage 41: Richard had picked stones out of the play court and threw one in the dayroom, breaking a window. There was no reason for his action, only to create excitement.

3. May 6, 1962, 5:30 p.m., Cottage 41: Richard sneaked out of the dining room tonight before supper was over and hid out on the far side of the play court. His actions had the other boys shouting and excited, as usual. When I brought him in and told him he was to sit, he threw a temper tantrum, striking, kicking and swearing at me. He was secluded until 8 p.m. Richard is a constant behavior problem. He has an uncanny way of causing complete havoc in this ward and delights in doing so.

4. Aug. 19, 1965, 8 p.m., Cottage 41: Richard became very difficult to handle. He started hitting and slapping several patients. He said he was going to run away again tonight. Richard was placed in seclusion for his protection and the protection of the other patients.

Killing Time

You just never knew when you might get your block knocked off. Most of the attendants were OK, but some liked to abuse us. I remember one who used a plastic baseball bat. Another one liked to knee the residents in the groin. You'd better do what you were told — that's for sure. You'd better not mess with those guys, or you'd be sorry. That's for sure.

— Richard Prangley

In the early days in Cottage 41, the fear and confusion gradually settled into a profound loneliness and a monotony more numbing than the tranquilizers.

Richard desperately needed a friend, but relationships in the normal sense were not possible in Cottage 41. There was too much insecurity and distrust — too much unpredictability in the behavior of the boys. Richard never knew when one of his fellow residents might take a swing at him for no apparent reason. He had to be on guard all the time.

The important thing to know wasn't how to make friends, but how to duck quickly. Popularity didn't matter. Being accepted and included didn't matter, either, because there was nothing to be included in. There was no "in" group, no cliques. Each resident was an individual; everybody was an outsider. There was one common goal: survival. But everybody pursued it individually. Like all the other boys of Cottage 41, Richard found his own formula for getting from one day to the next. Sporadic entries in his records from Coldwater offer glimpses of his first year there:

1. April 11, 1957: INTERVIEW: Parents in the office inquiring regarding the progress of the boy and what has happened to him since their last visit. They expressed satisfaction with the progress the boy has made since he came here.
2. May 16, 1957: ACCIDENT: Richard threw a stone striking [another boy] on the nose, causing a small laceration. Form "A."
3. Sept. 11, 1957: OFF GROUNDS on hike to root beer stand, accompanied by attendants

4. Sept. 27, 1957: INJURY: Richard sustained a black eye while playing. Form "A."
5. Nov. 23, 1957: BEHAVIOR: Richard kicked or hit [another resident] in the eye, causing a bruise. Form "A."
6. Dec. 23, 1957: OFF GROUNDS: Christmas shopping, accompanied by attendants.

For the next 15 years, Richard would have no real friends. Now and then somebody would come along and toss an act of kindness Richard's way. There was the female attendant who wiped away his tears when he cried to go home and sometimes slipped Richard a teddy bear to keep him company on those nights when his grief kept him awake. There was the recreation director who helped Richard learn to catch fly balls and build campfires. There was the psychologist who saw something in Richard nobody else had seen and took the trouble to persuade Richard's supervisors to take a second look at his placement in custodial care.

Richard met boys along the way who shared his sense of mischief. Richard and Steven both liked to sneak into the staff offices and steal candy bars. Richard and Kevin both liked to stand in the play court and kick balls onto the roof of Cottage 41. But Richard never considered sharing his feelings with these boys. He wouldn't think of telling the boys in Cottage 41 how he felt about not being able to go home or not seeing his parents more often. He never talked about his fears and dreams. Those were things Richard kept to himself. Like all the other boys, he shuffled through the routine of life at Cottage 41.

From Monday through Sunday, the boys rose at 6 a.m. The attendants brought them their clothes from another room. The boys lined up and walked to the dining hall. Their breakfast — usually oatmeal — was arranged on long wooden tables, waiting for them. Whatever the meal, the boys used only spoons — no knives or forks. The plates, bowls and cups were metal.

After breakfast, Richard and the other boys too young or too disabled to do even the simplest work, were herded into the dayroom, where they merely waited for the hours to tick by. Sometimes the attendants brought in balls, toys and puzzles. Occasionally, a book or two found its way into the dayroom, where it would be immediately torn to pieces. Paper was simply too tempting to the destructive impulses of the more violent boys.

There was a black and white television on one wall, but because these were the days before cable and daytime TV, the set was dark during the day. On Saturday mornings, the boys watched *Mighty Mouse* and *The Lone Ranger;* in the evenings, *Rin Tin Tin* and *Lassie.* Later, the boys gathered to marvel at 1960s sitcoms, which depicted lives as alien to the boys as Richard's favorite show of the 1960s, *Lost in Space.*

If the weather was decent, the boys might be taken out into the play court for outdoor recreation. Here they found fresh air and a release for their energy. There were swings and monkey bars and a teeter-totter. There was a patch of concrete and a basketball hoop. In the summer, the boys ran through a sprinkler. In the winter, they slid down a hill between the cottages on sleds and saucers. Richard particularly liked the baseball games pitting one cottage against another cottage. The downspout of the eaves trough was first base, the basketball-hoop pole was second base, and the teeter-totter was third base.

Now and then, attendants showed up with their arms full of skates — roller skates in the summer and ice skates in the winter — and the kids who were able to stand up on skates scrambled for pairs that fit. There were Friday afternoon movies in the dining hall — westerns and cartoons, mainly, on 16 mm film. Sometimes the boys were treated to rock 'n' roll on an old record player. They jumped and wriggled to the songs of Elvis Presley and Frankie Avalon, along with those of a young singer Richard especially liked, largely because of his name: Ricky Nelson.

There was square dancing (the boys never knew that girls generally played a role in that activity) and sing-alongs, hikes and sometimes even camp-outs — but never overnight — in the woods around the compound. The smell of coffee brewing on an open fire turned Richard into a coffee drinker when he was still in his early teens. After that, the smell of coffee always would remind him of those campfires in the woods near Coldwater and the illusion of freedom they created. It was one of his few happy memories of the institution.

At lunchtime, it was back to the dining hall, then back to the dayroom, then back to the dining hall for supper and, once again, back to the dayroom, where the boys would pass the hours until bedtime. The bathroom had only one shower. Three or four times a week, an attendant attached a garden hose to the shower head, and all the boys were stripped and lined up outside the shower stall. One attendant soaped the boys up; another hosed them down; a third slipped nightgowns over their heads.

The dormitory consisted of 40 metal beds arranged in four rows, and nothing more. At 8:30 p.m., while the attendants were tying the chronic roamers into their bunks, Richard would climb beneath his blanket and hope that he would be left alone until morning. He would have prayed to be left alone, except he didn't know about God — at least not the God that comforted the fearful.

Richard spent his earliest days in a Catholic household, where he had seen religious artifacts — the crucifix on the wall in his parents' bedroom, the oval-framed picture of a long-haired, bearded man who wore an expression of sincerity. They called him Jesus. One of the attendants at Coldwater had a photo of the same man in his office. Richard figured the man must be famous.

The younger kids in the institution got all their religion in the dayroom. For a couple of hours on Sunday afternoons, two attendants would insist that all the residents line up on the wooden benches. Then they'd wheel in the record player from the recreation room and play church songs. The kids who could remember lyrics and sing joined in on the old standards — "Do, Lord; do, Lord; do remember me …"

Sometimes the attendants would pass out pamphlets to the residents. Some of the pamphlets included photographs. That's where Richard saw him again — the long-haired man with the serene expression. There were no sermons in the dayroom, but now and then an attendant would be moved to tell the kids about heaven and the only way to get there — by behaving well and obeying orders. Maybe it was something spoken during one of these sessions, or maybe it was something Richard saw on TV, that led him to the concept of a creator — a supreme being who created the clouds and stars and kept an eye on the activities of human beings.

The way Richard understood it, God was aware of everything that was happening on earth. What's more, he could actually make things happen. Anything he wanted. Richard could use a friend like that.

Once Richard entered adolescence, he was allowed to attend church services in the gymnasium of the schoolhouse on the Coldwater grounds. The attendants wheeled in a portable altar. The Catholic services were on Saturday; the Protestant services on Sunday. Richard started going on Sundays until a staff member happened to notice in his records that he had come from a Catholic background. Then he started going on both Saturdays and Sundays — when, that is, the attendants at Cottage 41 allowed him to go.

Richard's parents sent him a rosary and a prayer book. He had no idea how to use the rosary and he couldn't read. Still, Richard enjoyed the singing and the ritual he observed at the services. He liked the idea of getting dressed up in his best clothes. He especially liked wearing a necktie — until one particular Sunday morning.

Richard was about 12. He was returning from services when an attendant ordered him to take part immediately in a particularly dirty job — helping out with the residents who weren't toilet trained. Richard, who didn't want to get his best clothes soiled, refused to do what the attendant told him. The attendant grabbed Richard's necktie and choked him until he gasped for air.

This experience would haunt Richard for the rest of his life. Perhaps because he had struggled for oxygen during his torturous journey down the birth canal, he had always exhibited an extreme sensitivity — a terror, in fact — toward having his breathing restricted. When he was a toddler, his parents could hardly get a shirt over Richard's head.

It was no wonder that the necktie episode left such an impression on him. Every time he tried to put on a necktie thereafter, he would feel the guard's hands on him and the loop getting tighter and tighter around his neck, choking off his breath. Even 20 years later, when he was invited to the White House, Richard couldn't bring himself to wear a tie. In fact, the only time he was able to force himself to put on a tie was to go to dinner at his parents' house after he was released from Coldwater. It was a real testament to the extent to which he sought their love and acceptance.

And so it went. Day after day, week after week, month after month. Richard's young mind — a mind not nearly as crippled as everybody presumed — was left to wander aimlessly, bumping up against life lessons wherever it could find them. At an age when most children are soaking up knowledge and experience, Richard was left to vegetate in the Cottage 41 dayroom, confused, abandoned and tranquilized. Still, he managed to figure out what he needed to survive.

1. March 3, 1958: MEDICAL NOTE: Richard was transferred to the isolation ward in Cottage 41 for observation of diarrhea.
2. June 2, 1958: BEHAVIOR: Richard found a paper clip which he straightened out, then scratched an eight-inch mark on [another resident's] back. Form "A" filed.
3. June 1, 1959: INJURY: Richard accidentally shut a door on his left finger, sustained a minor laceration.
4. Nov. 30, 1959: OUT FOR PLEASURE with father John Prangley.

The primary lesson at Cottage 41 was self-defense. Richard spent every hour of every day in the company of impulsive, unpredictable kids — kids who might punch him or kick him or bite him at any time, without provocation. If he was going to make it in this place, he would have to learn how to punch and kick and bite back.

Second, there was the moral code. Again, it had more to do with self-preservation than with right and wrong. To do something that displeased the attendants could lead to a knee in his stomach or a mop handle over his head or a leather belt across his legs. Sometimes the boys who misbehaved were forced to spend a day or two dressed only in shorts — no shirt, shoes or socks. There was no good and bad in the moral sense. Behavior that angered the attendants was to be avoided. Everything else was OK.

Formal allegations of abuse were leveled from time to time against the Coldwater State Home and Training School, but they never amounted to much.

On Oct. 8, 1958, about 2 ½ years after Richard went to Coldwater, a 45-year-old man named Joseph Kibiloski died two weeks after being admitted to the institution. Kibiloski's death was officially attributed to kidney disease; however, broken ribs and abrasions on his body at the time of his death caused some to suspect that physical abuse might have contributed to his death. A committee of the Michigan House of Representatives, assisted by the state police, conducted an investigation. In late October, the Branch County prosecutor issued a report stating he found no evidence for charges that mistreatment led to Kibiloski's death.

But State Rep. Harry J. Phillips, head of the legislative committee, refused to drop the investigation. Phillips had testimony from one eyewitness who said Kibiloski had been thrown "like a sack of potatoes" into a station wagon shortly before he died. Phillips convinced the state police to conduct polygraph tests on staff members who were giving conflicting statements in the case. But the day after Phillips vowed to continue the probe, a key witness, who was a Coldwater attendant, shot himself to death. The man had been one of the attendants who helped load Kibiloski into the station wagon.

In November, the state Mental Health Commission upheld the ruling of the Branch County prosecutor — that there was no evidence of criminal wrongdoing — and criticized Phillips's methods. The commission's report said, in part:

> Those who conduct such reviews and investigations have a responsibility to do so in a calm, objective and thorough manner, but premature accusations based on emotionalism rather than fact is the essential difference between destructive, as opposed to constructive, investigation.
>
> It is tragic to frighten the public and undermine its confidence in our mental hospitals by overpublicizing those instances where mistreatment is alleged and not confirmed. The very great distress, even panic, that such action creates in the families and relatives of our more than 30,000 patients is both unwarranted and inexcusable.

Then the commission's report took a curious turn. It went on to say that Kibiloski, who had trouble walking, "on several occasions had to be carried up and down stairs by *working patients* because of a shortage of attendants."

Then this: "One of these working patients is a very aggressive and, at times, assaultive individual, and it is alleged by other patients that he did, on one occasion, physically attack patient Kibiloski. This may or may not be true."

Aside from mentioning the "shortage of attendants," the commission didn't address the question of why Coldwater would assign an "aggressive and, at times, assaultive" person to carry another patient up and down stairs.

Fueled by additional reports of Coldwater patients coming home for Christmas that year with bruises and welts on their bodies, Phillips, defying the commission's report, continued to press on. Some believed that Phillips was grandstanding at the cost of the Coldwater staff. In fact, some citizens of the city of Coldwater felt that the allegations Phillips was tossing around were beginning to give their hometown a bad name. In January 1959, a delegation of 30 Coldwater civic leaders paid a visit to the Capitol in Lansing, Michigan. Their stated objectives were to defend the good name of the Coldwater State Home and Training School and to prevent the reappointment of Phillips as chairman of a House committee conducting the investigation.

According to a Coldwater alderman, "There was no need for an investigation of the type and caliber we had at Coldwater."

The legislators who represented Coldwater agreed.

"I would say Mr. Phillips made some rather intemperate and ill-advised statements," said Sen. John P. Smeekens.

The delegation had come to the Capitol armed with testimonials from various organizations and individuals in Coldwater. The local ministerial association wrote: "By all means, correct any abuses that are found by a quiet, efficient and thorough investigation. However, wait until the case has been investigated and charges found to be true before giving the 'news' to press, radio and TV."

The ministers said they had been besieged by parents making frantic appeals to find out if the charges of abuse were true.

A woman who toured the institution wrote: "If the Lord had seen fit to give me a child like those [in the institution], I would feel that I would be lacking as a parent and a human being if I didn't do everything possible to have him admitted to Coldwater State Home, for only there would he find his fulfillment."

Representative Phillips was not reappointed to head the legislative committee.

In August 1963, one resident of the institution — an 8-year-old Jackson boy — died of abdominal hemorrhaging after being beaten by another resident, a 15-year-old boy. Coldwater Superintendent Rennell called it "a very regrettable incident which might have been prevented if we had sufficient employees to give minute-to-minute supervision of every patient."

Two years later, a 24-year-old resident died of a "sharp blow to the liver," supposedly after a "scuffle" with another patient. A six-member coroner's jury ruled that the death was "unnatural, but not unlawful." Calling for an investigation of the death, State Sen. Raymond Dzendel of Detroit said: "If incidents like this occur because we don't have enough people, then we legislators must take the blame; if it is because there are attendants who don't belong there, then we should get rid of them."

Newspaper accounts of the episode end there.

Meanwhile, Richard was getting into some scuffles of his own. It was the way of life inside the institution. Incident after incident of physical confrontations were documented. Fistfights; cuts and bruises; fits of rage. They were all part of the daily routine at Coldwater.

It was no wonder Richard learned early how to cover up. But another lesson — one that worked its way into Richard's mind slowly, like a parasitic worm — was the most painful lesson of all. The attendants were right. His old home was gone forever.

All along, Richard saw other residents going home with their parents. He never understood why he didn't get to go home, too. It was a question he would wrestle with for the rest of his life — forever desperate for an answer.

That desperate yearning defined Richard's life at Coldwater. A year or so after he arrived at the institution, he prevailed upon an attendant to help him compose a letter to his parents begging for them to come and get him. He never received a reply. He never knew if the attendant ever mailed the letter, or even if he took down Richard's words.

At his former home, the Prangley family was growing prodigiously. Three boys arrived — in December 1956, March 1958, May 1959 — and a girl in June 1960. By the time Richard marked his fourth year in the institution, he had 10 brothers and sisters.

The family had moved to Grandville, which was only a few miles from Jenison. As if his children and job weren't enough to keep him busy, John ran for the Grandville City Council and was elected in 1965. He would later become mayor of the city, serving in that capacity from 1971 until 1977. The visits to Coldwater were tapering off. For whatever reason, John and Dorothy Prangley were distancing themselves from their son.

As Richard saw it, his parents were reinventing their family to exclude him. In his 15 years at Coldwater, Richard never went home once. Not even at Christmas, when — out of sentimentality, if for no other reason — even most of the hardest cases were welcomed, for a day or two, anyway, back into their families. It wasn't unusual for a resident to go home for 30 days at Christmastime.

Over the years, Richard asked frequently why he never got to go home. He heard various explanations. He was too unruly. His parents already had their hands full with all the other children. His poor behavior disallowed him the privilege of going home. But he never knew which reason, or excuse, was true.

On Christmas morning, the few residents left behind waited in the day-room after breakfast while the attendants unlucky enough to catch a Christmas Day shift would wheel in a cart of gifts. Most of them came from the parents of the residents. For the truly forgotten kids, there was the standard present from the State of Michigan — a cardboard core from a toilet paper roll stuffed with hard candy.

It didn't matter much which child got the toilet paper rolls and which got the gifts. For the most part, there were no individual possessions for the residents of Cottage 41. If a resident got a new sweater or jacket or pair of pajamas, it would be kept in the clothing room for him. But the boys weren't allowed to keep their toys. On the evening of Dec. 25, all the Christmas toys, those that couldn't be used as weapons, anyway, went into the common toy bin. Most of them were destroyed in a matter of days. Those sturdy enough to withstand intensive abuse became communal property.

Richard did have one prized possession during his stay at Coldwater, at least for a little while. In 1963, he was approaching his 14th birthday and had become a full-fledged "working boy," the unofficial title given to the boys who were trusted with small jobs on the Coldwater grounds — mostly maintenance chores. For months, he lobbied his parents to bring him a wristwatch. It would make him feel more grown-up, more important. In a letter to the Coldwater staff dated Nov. 28, 1963, John Prangley apologized for not coming more often and informed the staff that he planned to be there for Richard's birthday. He wrote: "We would like to get a little Timex watch. He always mentions one when we see him, and we were wondering if he would be allowed to have it."

The director of Social Services replied: "I am sure he would be happy to receive a wrist watch, but I must caution you that it will be necessary for you to sign a release of responsibility in order that the institution may not be held responsible in case of damage to the article."

Richard got his watch. He had it for four days before another resident snatched it from him and smashed it. In horror, Richard watched the pieces of his watch fly across the cottage floor. But he expected neither restitution nor sympathy. The attendants were right; inside Coldwater, each possession was just another loss that hadn't happened yet.

A lost watch was by no means Richard's biggest heartbreak. Almost from his first day at Coldwater, he could feel that his family was slipping through his fingers. The records show that after the first visit in July 1956, John and Dorothy Prangley came again two months later. Then, on Nov. 30, the day before Richard's birthday, John Prangley brought Richard's grandmother with him. The Prangleys visited Richard three times in 1957 — in April, June and November. They skipped 1958 entirely. On Nov. 30, 1959, the day before Richard turned 10, John Prangley came alone. A year later, both parents came.

Evidently, John Prangley felt guilty about the dwindling contact with his son. On Nov. 18, 1962, after nearly two years had passed without a visit to Coldwater, he wrote to the director of the institution's Social Service Department:

> I hardly know what to write in my letter to you. I'm truly sorry we haven't written before, or been down to the school to see our son, Richard. We sincerely didn't wish it to be this way.
>
> Why? I really can't answer. We didn't want to neglect our obligations. We planned so many times to come. Right now, we plan to come on Monday, Nov. 26. We plan on arriving about noon time and would like to take Richard out for lunch. We are mailing a winter jacket this week and would like to know what other clothing he is in need of, so we could bring them with us. If possible, please write and let us know.

We would like to see you also and explain the situation we have. We are truly sorry we haven't done our part. We have prayed awful hard.

On Nov. 26, eight days after he wrote that letter, John came to Coldwater alone.

One year later, on Nov. 28, 1963, three days before Richard turned 14, John Prangley wrote again: "I'm writing this letter to inquire about the present condition of our son, Richard Leigh. Having a large family here at home and the distance we are from him, we sometimes take too much for granted. But we are concerned and do pray each day for his happiness."

Both parents came to Coldwater on Dec. 9, 1963, then in August 1964. John came by himself on Dec. 13, 1965. If the records are correct, that was the last time either of the parents made the trip to Coldwater.

As for written correspondence, the records show that between 1960 and 1970, Richard received 70 letters and cards from his parents, siblings and other relatives and friends. He always managed to find an attendant willing to take the time to read them to him.

But, like the visits, the cards and letters tapered off over the years. The records show that after 1965 Richard received only 12 cards and letters.

Regardless of how long it had been since the previous visit, Richard was always happy to see his parents. It was, if nothing else, a blessed break in the routine, and it always felt good to get off the Coldwater grounds.

An attendant would come into the ward and tell Richard his parents were there and that he was going "off the grounds for pleasure." That was the official phrase: "off the grounds for pleasure." The attendant would take Richard to the clothes room and dress him in his best clothes. Then he would take him to the front door of Cottage 41, where his parents would be waiting for him. Sometimes one or two brothers and sisters would accompany John and Dorothy. Never all of them, of course. By then, there were too many. They usually went to Mac's Restaurant in downtown Coldwater for a lunch or dinner that invariably left everybody feeling bad.

The conversation always took the same turn. Maybe that's why the visits became so painful for John and Dorothy Prangley. Maybe it was why they quit coming. For the longest time, Richard didn't get it. It was always the same question: When were his parents going to take him home? The answers, on the other hand, underwent a kind of evolution — from "One of these days," to "When you get better," to "We have so many kids at home already." At that point in Richard's life, such answers only added to his general sense of confusion over the cruel turn his life had taken since that long car ride to Coldwater in June 1956. It was only much later in life that he was able to articulate the facts of the matter:

"By then I wasn't part of the family any more; I belonged to the state," Richard said. "My home was Coldwater and my real parent was the mental health system."

The fact was that Richard could no longer expect anything from his parents. He was out of their jurisdiction. He was an orphan whose parents were still alive.

In adolescence, the lessons got more difficult; survival became more complicated than just punching back and avoiding the wrath of the attendants. When Richard was 12, he was roused from sleep in the middle of the night. Somebody was climbing into bed with him. Somebody was rolling Richard onto his stomach, then climbing on top of him. He couldn't make out the face in the darkness, but he recognized the voice. It was a boy in Cottage 41 who was three years older than Richard. The boy hissed into Richard's ear that if he made any noise, he would beat the crap out of him.

Richard had only the vaguest idea of what was happening. He had heard the term "bed-hoppers." He had heard the talk about older boys in the ward who crawled into bed with other boys in the middle of the night and "played dirty" with them. Richard didn't know what it was, or why they did it. It was some kind of game, he guessed. He didn't care what or why. It was best not to ask too many questions. They could do what they wanted just as long as they stayed out of his bed. The space between his sheet and his blanket was the only place on earth he could call his own. It was the only place he had any peace.

Richard felt the boy's hands groping for the bottom hem of his nightshirt, then he felt the boy pulling the nightshirt up, over his private parts. Richard gasped as he felt the boy's penis probe between his legs.

Richard refused to cooperate. He would keep quiet to avoid a beating, but that was as far as he would go. He would not let the boy penetrate him. After a few seconds of bouncing and shuddering and gasping into Richard's ear, the boy was done with whatever he had been doing. He just went limp all of a sudden. Before he went back to his own bed, the boy repeated his warning. If Richard told the attendants about this, the boy would knock his block off.

Unable to go back to sleep, Richard lay awake in the darkness. His buttocks were covered with the sticky bodily fluid the boys in the ward called "jazz." He couldn't even get up to wash because the night attendant might see him and start asking questions. So Richard remained in bed, wide awake with the boy's jazz all over his back, his nightshirt and his sheet. It was a long night, a night in which Richard would have more than enough time to think about how his bed never would be the same.

He was right; his bed never *was* the same. The middle-of-the-night violations became part of the routine of life in Cottage 41. Sometimes the rapists would take Richard into the bathroom and make a party out of it. Richard wasn't the only victim. The smaller, better-looking boys had it worse than he did.

But they kept their mouths shut, too. Everybody did. That's how you survived in Cottage 41. And when you couldn't take it anymore, you ran away, even though escapes from Coldwater were notoriously futile and short-lived.

During a four-month period in 1965, Richard was involved in two "escapes." In May, he made it to a farmhouse just a mile or so from the institution. The owner of the house called the attendants, and Richard was back in Cottage 41 less than one hour after he was reported missing. Later that summer, attendants reported Richard as an escapee, but soon found him hiding in a park behind Cottage 41.

Adolescence awakened in Richard two conflicting forces. First came a rebelliousness that got him into trouble. In the early- to mid-1960s, as Richard was coming of age, he became what the attendants at Coldwater described as a "behavior problem." He got into fights. He showed up at meals with unexplained injuries. He escaped from the compound twice and constantly threatened to go again. He spent many hours during those years in forced "seclusion," a euphemism for solitary confinement. During those years, his progress reports were peppered with such phrases as, "very destructive, lies and steals;" "a very aggressive boy;" and "Richard's biggest trouble is that he talks constantly."

But Richard also suddenly developed a certain competency, a usefulness, that seemed to spring from nowhere.

Richard Prangley's "progress sheets" provided a capsulated report of what he did each month while inside the institution. The records documented his weight, health, behavior, transfers, medications, activities and work assignments.

Throughout the first 11 years, the activities were always the same: TV, movies, recreation, church and play (sometimes play *class;* sometimes play *therapy*). Translation: Richard was vegetating in the dayroom nearly all of his waking hours.

Before April 1963, the entry for "work assignment" was always "none." But for that month the entry says: "Feed, ward work." That meant that Richard, at age 14, was at last doing something useful in his life. He was helping to feed those who were even worse off than himself, and he was mopping up their mistakes.

The attendants had began to notice — to their profound surprise — that Richard was capable of following through, of sticking with a job until it was finished. The kid could follow orders. He was strong and energetic. He was conscientious; sometimes even meticulous. And — this was the real shock — he could figure out a few things on his own. Simple things, of course, but still ... a boy like that was a valuable commodity at Coldwater, where the unpleasant tasks never ended.

Soon Richard was a full-fledged "working boy." That was the term used by the attendants, and the residents themselves, for the boys who were given chores each day. They were janitors, mopping and scrubbing and sweeping the ward, mopping up feces and stripping beds of urine-soaked sheets. They were kitchen assistants, washing dishes and scouring pans. They were doers of the dirty work, changing diapers, feeding those who couldn't lift their own spoons and "stooling the low-grades."

It worked like this: Each of the four wards in Cottage 41 had a bathroom, and each bathroom had a row of five commodes. Several times a day, the attendants or, more often, the "working boys" at the bottom of the pecking order, would herd the residents who weren't toilet trained into the bathroom and line them up at the commodes. In order to speed the process along, the "low-grades" were forced to double up on the commodes. Literally, two residents would use the same stool simultaneously. Part of the job was to clean up anything that missed the target. There was always a lot that missed the target.

Richard was "stooling the low-grades," in fact, on that afternoon of Nov. 22, 1963, when, on the verge of turning 14, he heard about the assassination of John F. Kennedy. It didn't mean much to Richard, but he could tell by the behavior of the attendants that it was major event in the outside world. That's how he recalls the event, reflected off the faces of the attendants, as he was stooling the low-grades.

In some ways, it was better than hanging out all day with the aimless, volatile population of the dayroom. On the other hand, the working boys couldn't help but notice that they were doing all the worst jobs, the jobs that the staff didn't want to do. But it was the staff that was getting paid, not the working boys.

The working boys could grumble that the arrangement was unfair, but what could they do about it? Form a union? Go on strike? Quit? Richard's answer, as he entered his teenage years was to mouth off, refuse to do the work, throw a tantrum, or run away. But he had nowhere to go. And all it got him anyway was another black eye or split lip, and another night of "seclusion."

In the end, the dirty work still was there. So were the attendants, holding all the cards, calling all the shots.

On the other hand, there were small rewards for the working boys who did what they were told to do and kept their mouths shut. A candy bar here and there. Extended TV privileges at night. And, best of all, freedom from abuse. Gradually, Richard learned one more lesson: going along to get along.

Compromise? Surrender? It didn't matter how you described it. Richard came to realize that, when all was said and done, he was going to end up in the same place anyway. He might as well take the smoothest path.

The staff called it "work experience." The residents called it exploitation. Either way, it went beyond the fences of Coldwater. Beginning in July 1968, Richard started going on a series of weeklong vacations to the home of one particular member of the Coldwater staff. In the beginning, Richard loved the vacations. It was a genuine holiday just to sleep in a real home and eat home-cooked meals with a real family. There were no curfews and no punches to dodge. The occasional day trips to parks and shopping malls and county fairs were a bonus. But gradually Richard began to notice that the bonuses tapered off, while the work just kept piling up.

When it came right down to it, the so-called vacations were nearly all work. Most of the time, Richard was scrubbing floors, washing windows, mowing grass, or pulling soggy leaves from eaves troughs — first in the home of his primary host and later at the home of the host's friend. As much as he appreciated the opportunity to taste life outside Coldwater, Richard sensed that there was something cockeyed in the relationship — that he was being taken advantage of. Yet, he continued to go on the vacations for the next two years.

Richard was discovering, more and more as time went on, that his physical abilities could lead to his best shot at life in the outside world. The price of his ticket back into the real world, it seemed, was the sweat of his brow and his singleminded devotion to finish the tasks he started, however lowly they were.

Moving Up

Some guys at Cottage 14 tried some stuff. I wasn't going to put up with it.
I had enough of that monkey business back at Cottage 41. I wasn't going to
put up with any more of it.

— Richard Prangley

Richard worked his way out of Cottage 41 — literally. His thoroughness and reliability as a working boy earned him grudging respect from the attendants, which, in turn, diminished his urge to strike out. Slowly, Richard's reputation as "a behavior problem" faded. Maybe he wasn't a complete throwaway, after all. Maybe there was something in Richard Prangley that made him salvageable. Richard tried to run away from Cottage 41 and failed. Finally, he realized the only way out was along the uphill path chosen by those in charge. So, Richard climbed out, inch by inch. But it was by no means a smooth ascension.

Although he had spent a brief period in a cottage for higher-functioning children, Richard literally grew up in Cottage 41, the bottom rung of the institutional ladder. It wasn't until Sept. 16, 1966, when Richard, 2 ½ months short of his 18th birthday, was transferred to Cottage 42 for a "special educational project." A letter to John and Dorothy Prangley from the director of Social Services explained: "Your son is participating in a special training program in Cottage 42. As a means of measuring and documenting progress of the patients in this program, motion pictures are to be taken periodically of the children in their various activities. It is probable that these pictures will be shown from time to time before various interested groups."

The records offer no explanation for the sudden faith in Richard's ability to function in an environment beyond the custodial stage. It provides no evidence to support the belief that Richard was ready for a new challenge. On Dec. 3, 1965, just nine months before he was transferred to Cottage 42, Richard, now 16, was examined once again. The diagnosis this time was: "Mental deficiency; imbecile. Recommendation: Continued cottage care."

Perhaps one explanation for the move was that the people in charge at Coldwater were beginning to respond to society's gradually shifting philosophy against warehousing people like Richard. Maybe Richard's newfound confidence as a working boy persuaded the staff to give him another chance to prove himself. After all, he was on the verge of his 18th birthday. If Richard was ever going to be anything other than a burden on society, it was now or never.

For whatever reason, Richard was plucked from Cottage 41 and deposited in Cottage 42, where he spent a year and 10 months. Cottage 42 was as crowded as Cottage 41, but the expectations were slightly higher for the residents there, and the opportunities were a little richer. The boys received rudimentary vocational training. A lot of it was on-the-job janitorial training, which wasn't much different than what Richard had been doing in Cottage 41. On the other hand, the boys in Cottage 42 had access to a woodworking shop, and they attended classes where they learned the alphabet and basic math. They listened to lectures on how to hold down jobs on the outside. And residents of Cottage 42 were a little freer to move around the Coldwater grounds.

Richard did so well in Cottage 42 that his next transfer, in May 1968, was to Cottage 14, a unit for 50 to 60 high-functioning young adults. Richard, nearly 19, spent his days in Cottage 14 doing actual work on the Coldwater grounds, work other than cleaning up after other people. He repaired windows and plastered walls and performed other maintenance and groundskeeping tasks, working alongside the paid staff. Richard liked the days at Cottage 14. He liked doing work that didn't involve a mop, work that allowed him to actually accomplish something. And working with the paid staff, he was learning how to use his hands for something other than janitorial work.

But the nights were a different story. The sexual abuse that had been a routine part of life in Cottage 41 was almost nonexistent in Cottage 42, where Richard actually grew accustomed to sleeping through the night. Cottage 14, on the other hand, was a rude awakening. The difference was that Richard was much older and more experienced; he had some newfound self-respect under his belt and some new muscle. He wasn't about to go quietly this time.

Richard let it be known that he would not tolerate the advances of the bed-hoppers in Cottage 14. When his verbal warnings didn't work, he fought back with his fists. It was a losing battle; he was outnumbered. And so Richard committed the ultimate prison-mentality sin, he told the attendants what was going on. This only earned him more beatings. Soon his situation was not only intolerable, but dangerous, as well.

After three months in Cottage 14, Richard was ready to go back to Cottage 42. He didn't care if it was a step backward. He didn't even care if it meant that he would return to mop duty. He just wanted to be left alone. He just wanted his dignity back — and his bed.

His requests for a transfer back to Cottage 42 were ignored. Desperate to put an end to the abuse, he returned to Cottage 42 on his own, without anybody's permission. As the staff saw it, Richard had escaped a third time, even though he never left the grounds. That act of defiance — from Richard's view, of course, it was self-preservation, not defiance — would land him at the very bottom of his life at Coldwater: Cottage 19.

A note entered into his records on Sept. 8, 1968 described the episode this way: "Richard was found near Cottage 42, where he had gone without permission. He was picked up and taken to Cottage 19 by the Safety Department. Following his admission to Cottage 19, he was very upset and was placed in seclusion, until he became more calm."

On the following day, something called the Cottage 19 Review Committee Report also became part of Richard's permanent record. It said: "Richard Prangley is adjusting at a decidedly low level and was previously placed in Cottage 14 in an effort to see if he could adjust to the comparative freedom of an open cottage. However, his adjustment has been sufficiently poor to justify his recent transfer to Cottage 19."

Cottage 19 was for hardcore behavior problems. It was called the "lockup cottage" and was essentially a maximum-security prison within a minimum-security prison. For Richard's welcome to Cottage 19, he was ordered to strip and step into a shower stall where his entire body was sprayed with a liquid disinfectant known by the residents as "crab dope." After taking a shower, Richard, still naked, was led to a cell with concrete walls and steel doors.

There, two attendants established the tone of Cottage 19 by working Richard over. They punched and kicked him and repeatedly shoved his head against a wall. Not enough to draw blood or render Richard unconscious, but just enough to let him know he was no longer in Cottage 14, or even Cottage 41. Richard was left in the cell overnight with nothing but a blanket. In the morning, an attendant shoved Richard's breakfast through a hole in the door.

After breakfast, he was given clothes and led to a courtyard. As he walked down the hallway, an attendant punched him once more, apparently just to refresh his memory about where he was. In the courtyard, Richard was shoved into a line of other residents doing calisthenics.

The two attendants supervising the pushups amused themselves with a cruel game. One of the attendants was named Brown. Repeatedly, the other attendant demanded that Richard tell him "the color of shit." Every time, Richard, his face to the ground, answered, "Brown." Pretending that Richard had insulted him, the attendant whose name was Brown stepped on Richard's neck and ground his face into the concrete. When Richard refused to answer the question, the other attendant put *his* foot on Richard's neck.

Mercifully, Richard's stay at Cottage 19 was brief. He never spent another night there. After his delousing, after his night in the concrete cell and his morning of calisthenics and humiliation, he was transferred back to Cottage 41. After his successes in Cottage 42, and the work he enjoyed while in Cottage 14, returning to 41 felt like a defeat. But anything was better than Cottage 19.

The backsliding, it so happened, was only temporary. In January 1969, Richard was sent, once again, to live among the higher-functioning residents. This time he was transferred to Cottage 12. Finally, he was on his way up for good. Two months before that transfer, a member of Coldwater's Psychology Department wrote this letter to his fellow staff members: "I have had contact recently with personnel in Cottage 41 and also friends of Richard who feel that he is capable of doing more than is presently available to him. I notice that at one time he was functioning in a line setting. I am wondering if he is not more capable than present tests show. Would it be possible to test his performance in some way, so that we would have a better idea of his capabilities?"

In December 1968, one day after Richard's 19th birthday, he was tested by a psychologist. The results of the test were astonishing. The psychologist described Prangley as "quite pleasant," "cooperative" and "well motivated." The psychologist wrote:

> According to his performance on the Weschler Adult Intelligence Scale, Richard has a Full Scale IQ of 70, which places him in the Borderline category, His Performance IQ falls near the upper limit of the Borderline range, significantly higher than his Verbal IQ, which is in the mild level of retardation.
>
> On the Verbal Scale, a relatively high Digit Span score indicates fairly good attention and concentration, while a score of zero on the Similarities tests shows little, if any, verbal conceptual ability.
>
> The results of this test indicate that Richard functions intellectually at the Borderline level with considerably better-developed nonverbal than verbal ability. This factor probably accounts for at least some of the discrepancy between present and previous tests results, as the Stanford-Binet is primarily a test of verbal and academic ability, whereas the Weschler is a test of nonverbal or performance ability as well. Thus the results of this test are more indicative of his overall functioning, of his nonverbal as well as his verbal ability....

Then the psychologist wrote a sentence that's absolutely heartbreaking in its casual dismissal of everything it implies, especially when read in the context of the 25 years that followed: "He certainly shows greater ability than we had estimated previously."

In other words, Richard never belonged in Cottage 41. Those early assessments that doomed him to a wasted youth were wrong. It took the Coldwater staff only 13 years to discover that.

The psychologist concluded: "This does suggest that he is capable of adjusting to a less restrictive and more competitive setting."

Two years later, one week before Richard turned 21, the same psychologist tested Richard again. The results reaffirmed the verdict of the previous test: Richard had been seriously underestimated all his life. Although he remained, as the psychologist put it, "defective" in reading, spelling and arithmetic, he was not the throwaway human being so many people thought he was. This time the psychologist wrote:

> The results of these tests indicate that Richard functions intellectually in the Mild range of mental retardation.... It appears that his assets include a friendly and cooperative attitude, and well-developed visual-motor coordination and control, which enables him to perform extremely well at some manual type tasks.
>
> I recommend speech therapy and perhaps some counseling to help him adjust to vocational training and/or job placement.

Richard had come a long way from "violent," "destructive," and "unmanageable," to "friendly and cooperative." From "low-grade moron" and "imbecile," to "mildly retarded." A long way, yes, but where would Richard have been one week before his 21st birthday if, instead of being locked up in custodial care at Coldwater, he had spent the previous 14 years in a nurturing environment?

Obviously, there was more to it than profound changes in Richard. There was, in fact, a profound change in the institution. In July of 1970, Dr. C. Dale Barrett Jr. took over as medical director at Coldwater. In a February 1971 interview, Barrett told the *Lansing* (Mich.) *State Journal* that 1970 had been a year of "dramatic and revolutionary change" at Coldwater. Barrett brought a revolutionary perspective to the job: He went in assuming that everybody in the institution had been underestimated. He planned to do away with pure custodial care. He was convinced, he said, that every retarded person had a higher level of capability than had been acknowledged in the past.

"It is my fervent belief that there is not a single retarded person residing at the institution who cannot be helped to achieve some higher level of skill or functioning," Barrett said.

He said he was committed to reducing the number of patients at Coldwater by at least 450 in 1971–72.

"Many of our residents at Coldwater do not belong here," he said. "They were placed here at a time when people believed that any retarded child naturally belonged in an institution."

That's why Richard suddenly became so smart in 1970.

Eight years later, Barrett would be undone by scandal involving the misuse of funds at the institution. An investigation by the auditor general would reveal a variety of improprieties. After briefly accepting a "demotion" from director to top medical officer, a demotion that would have given Barrett a $7,500-per-year pay raise, Barrett, under fire from both his staff and the state legislature, left the institution.

Richard might have spent the rest of his life brooding over the poor decisions that spoiled the first 20 years of his life. He might have decided to surrender to everybody's expectations. Who could blame him if he made it his mission to strike back at a world that discarded him when he was just a boy?

But Richard had no time for acrimony. He was too busy proving what the later tests showed and what he had known all along. In February 1969, while in Cottage 12, he was put on a vocational assignment, which eventually landed him in jobs off the grounds of Coldwater, one on a nearby farm and the other working maintenance with an engineering services company. He worked six days a week, eight hours a day — four as a farmhand and four as a janitor. Both enterprises were run by the same man. Asked to comment on Richard's value as a worker, here's what Richard's employer wrote in May 1971:

> He was employed by me for 1 ½ years … both on my farm and in my business.
>
> While employed on my farm, he fed and watered the livestock each day. He also performed general farm duties, such as building and painting fences, and assisted during the haying season. He was extremely conscientious and reliable in all duties which were given to him. After a short period of supervision, he was able to perform all assigned duties on his own with only minimal periodic assistance. He displayed an excellent memory and was always found to follow orders well in all situations.
>
> While employed in my business, he performed general janitorial and light maintenance duties. In this capacity, he was an excellent worker in all respects and was found to be honest and trustworthy. He regularly performed such duties as vacuuming the carpet, cleaning and waxing the floors, washing windows and burning the trash. He also performed light maintenance duties, such as the cleaning, sanding and repainting of equipment.
>
> Richard was always polite and respectful with all of his fellow workers and appeared to be well liked by them. I was sorry to see him leave our employ and would rehire him at any time should he be available.

On Dec. 4, 1970, three days after Richard turned 21, seven members of the Coldwater staff met for a "disposition conference." They decided that Richard was ready for release from Coldwater and that he was best suited to a "contract home," a small, privately run transitional group home. The one they had in mind was the Hanson Home of Grand Rapids, run by Mildred Hanson.[†]

While at the Hanson Home, Richard would be on convalescent status. The situation would be monitored by a social worker from the Kent County Consultation Center. The Richard Prangley case would be assigned to a caseworker named Eunice.

Later that month, a social worker at Coldwater named Gordon started paving the way for Richard's reentry into the world by writing to the caseworker.

"Richard is a very good resident of the institution," Gordon wrote. "He was inappropriately placed in a custodial cottage for some period of years and therefore has some speech mannerisms and social habits, such as sometimes interrupting inappropriately, that you would not normally expect from a resident of his intelligence level. He is usually cooperative and has a very positive attitude toward working and self-improvement."

There it was again, a casual reference to the terrible mistake: *He was inappropriately placed in a custodial care cottage for some period of years.*

On May 17, 1971, 14 years, 11 months and 13 days after Ricky Prangley, a scared, confused 6-year-old boy, was left on the doorstep of the Coldwater State Home and Training School, Richard Prangley, a 21-year-old man, walked out. The man was still a little scared and confused, but this time he felt a new emotion; this time he felt elation, not despair. Facing the exhilarating prospect of a life with real choices, a life free of the oppression of institutional life, he walked out of Coldwater with endless possibilities before him. The problem was he had virtually no equipment for sorting them out and choosing the right ones. One struggle was over; another struggle was about to begin.

The entry for that day in Richard's day-to-day activity report says: "May 17, 1971: Placed On Convalescent Status in the contract home of [Mrs. Hanson], Grand Rapids."

It was Richard's semi-independence day.

---

† The names of the home and owner have been changed to protect the owner's privacy.

Back in the World

They told me I was going to the Hanson Home in Grand Rapids. I wasn't exactly sure what that was, but I didn't care — as long as I was getting out of Coldwater. It had to be better than Coldwater. In Grand Rapids, I looked out the car window and saw the tall buildings and all the people walking around. That's when I started to get a little nervous.

— Richard Prangley

It was a sunny, unseasonably warm Monday in May. Social worker Gordon helped Richard load his belongings into the state-owned station wagon, then Gordon drove Richard the 100 miles to Grand Rapids, giving him a pep talk all the way. Gordon reminded Richard of the obstacles and temptations he would encounter on the outside. He told Richard about the people who would be eager to take advantage of him. To Richard, it didn't sound all that different from life on the inside. His mind was locked on a single concept: freedom.

Still, the heady confidence Richard felt when he walked out of Cottage 12 that morning began to fade a little as he saw the imposing buildings of downtown Grand Rapids, the second largest city in Michigan. Aside from a quick trip to Detroit to see the Tigers play while he was in the institution, Coldwater was the largest city Richard ever had seen. Grand Rapids was nothing like Coldwater. Grand Rapids was a real city, bursting with possibilities, and threats.

Richard saw the people in cars and on foot, going about their business among the imposing buildings, keeping their appointments and conducting their affairs. These were people who took their freedom and independence for granted. Richard wondered if he really would become one of them.

Would he one day be walking among those same buildings, on his way to a job or an appointment? Would he one day become so accustomed to independence that he would wear it so naturally? Everybody had been telling Richard that would take time. He was so eager to get started that he fidgeted in the front seat of the station wagon. All the way to Grand Rapids, Gordon was like a parole officer counseling an ex-con about the pitfalls of life on the outside. The big difference was that every ex-con had lived on the outside before. Richard hadn't.

The Hanson Home was also the Hanson *house,* a private residence not far from the heart of the city. Mrs. Hanson (the residents were never told her first name and never felt invited to inquire) was a short, middle-aged, businesslike widow who lived in the two-story house. She also, according to contract with the State of Michigan, provided shelter for four men at a time, former residents of institutions easing their way back into the real world.

Four men. Two bedrooms. Richard shared his with a man he had known vaguely in Cottage 12, where they never hit it off. Richard thought the man, who was about 10 years older, was a smart aleck. Having been in the room first, Richard's new roommate had things arranged his own way and wanted to keep them that way. Richard, the newcomer, had his work cut out for him.

Mrs. Hanson was a stickler for rules. The men could take showers only at certain times. They had to obey curfews. Mrs. Hanson demanded to know where the men were at all times, what time they left and what time they returned. She insisted on knowing what they bought, where they bought it and how much they paid for it. Mrs. Hanson was only doing her job, but, free, finally, from the authoritarianism of the institution, the last thing Richard wanted at that point in his life was somebody trying to manage the details of his life.

Richard's dissatisfaction with the arrangement quickly showed. Four months into his new life, Richard's caseworker, Eunice, wrote a long letter to the director of the outpatient department at Coldwater. Clearly Richard had his signals crossed. He knew he was going from Coldwater to something called a "group home," but he really didn't know what that meant. He thought he would enjoy much greater independence. He thought he would be free. According to the letter from Eunice,

> From the beginning, it was obvious that [Richard] did not understand his role in the [Hanson] Home or the purpose of convalescent status. He told me he thought he was coming to Grand Rapids to have his own apartment and to be completely independent of Coldwater.
>
> He brought with him a large milk can, several flower boxes, two large cabinets filled with dishes, pans, a Christmas tree, flags and several boxes of groceries. [Once he got out of Cottage 41, Richard was allowed to accumulate a few possessions, and he took full advantage of it.] Since there was no room to store these things, they were placed in the basement. This upset him very much since he wanted to keep all these things in his bedroom. Too, he resented the fact that he had to share a bedroom. He mentioned several times that he preferred the [Coldwater] exit cottage, where he had a private room.

Neither did he understand Mrs. Hanson's role in the family situation. He insisted he was going to prepare his own meals after the others ate. Needless to say, Mrs. Hanson could not allow each resident to do this, so he was firmly told that he must cooperate. He would disappear from home for many hours without telling anyone of his whereabouts. On two occasions, he was chased by a group of boys, and he called home for help. When this happened, Mrs. Hanson's assistant went to pick him up in his car.

According to the caseworker's letter, on May 27 Richard was accepted in a work-evaluation program at Pinerest Sheltered Workshop. He participated in the program there until June 30, when he was hired as a dietary aide at Butterworth Hospital. For $1.90 per hour, his duties were to mop the dining area and kitchen several times a day. He worked Monday through Friday from 11:45 a.m. to 8:15 p.m.

On the positive side, Richard's capacity for diligence on the job was serving him well. In fact, after only four months on the outside, he was already raising his sights.

Eunice wrote: "He is considered a good worker in this structured, routine job. However, he is not happy with the job and yesterday asked that I find him another since he does not like to work in the evening. This was discussed at great length. I feel he now understands the difficulty in finding jobs. I tried to emphasize that every job has some drawbacks. He was told that if he quits this job it will be up to him to find another. I am hopeful that the material things he has been able to purchase will be reward enough to give him the incentive to stay on the job."

To Richard, it was big money, nearly $80 a week, and every penny of it belonged to him. For 21 years, consumer goods had been off limits to him. He was carrying around a tremendous pent-up demand. Suddenly all the merchandise of the modern world was all right there, in the shops he passed as he walked the streets of Grand Rapids. Although Mrs. Hanson insisted that Richard start a savings account, his first couple of paychecks financed the shopping spree he had been denied all those years.

In her letter to Coldwater, Eunice provided a complete inventory: "He has thus far purchased a transistor radio, a wrist watch, a pocket watch, a clock, fishing equipment and a large cooler, plus some clothing. He was quite extravagant at first but has managed to control his impulsive buying somewhat since we threatened to take his bank book. Since Sept. 5 he has been paying full room and board."

As if trying to figure out his place in society weren't enough of a challenge for a young man emerging from a closet after 15 years, Richard was still trying to figure out where he stood with his family. Within hours after Richard arrived in Grand Rapids, he contacted his family. He called them at least once a day. His mother contacted the caseworker after several days and indicated she was apprehensive about seeing him after so many years. She made it clear that there was no room in their home for Richard, but he would be welcome to visit. In fact, Richard was invited to his parents' home for dinner three times and spent a week's vacation camping with the family during his first summer in Grand Rapids.

However, according to Eunice, "There has been no contact lately and Richard has expressed his anger toward [his parents] to [Mrs. Hanson]. We will continue to take an attitude of firm kindness with Richard. Hopefully, we will be able to work through problems as they arise."

Richard had, indeed, taken advantage of his first opening to reestablish ties with his parents. The day he landed in Grand Rapids, Mrs. Hanson, not one to waste time, sent him to the Pinerest Sheltered Workshop, which gave most of Hanson Home's new residents their first job, doing various kinds of piecework for 50 cents an hour. Richard's first assignment at Pinerest was assembling coat hangers, the same mindless task, hour after hour. Even so, he had plenty to think about. On the first coffee break of his first day at Pinerest, Richard made a beeline to the pay telephone and dialed a telephone number he had been carrying for months on a scrap of paper tucked into his wallet.

According to the records, neither John nor Dorothy Prangley visited Coldwater after December 1965, although they wrote to their son a half-dozen times after that. Even so, Richard didn't want to give up on them. He created excuses for them. What was the alternative? To accept the fact that his parents didn't want to see him anymore? That was unacceptable. Maybe, he figured, they would be more inclined to reestablish ties once he got out of the institution and became a regular person, leading a regular life, just like them.

Here's what he would do: He'd get out of Coldwater, get settled in the group home, then one day give them a buzz on the telephone and tell them he was living in Grand Rapids, just a few miles from the family home in Grandville. He wouldn't even mention Coldwater. There would be plenty of time to get around to that once they became comfortable with each other again.

In that first conversation, Richard would suggest they get together. After all, wasn't that the way people got in touch with each other on the outside? Wasn't that the way they socialized? Richard's parents would be so impressed with his sophistication, evident in his social skills and his use of the telephone, that they'd welcome him back into their lives with open arms. It would be like a scene from one of the movies Richard had seen of a son returning home from war. After all, he had been through a kind of war.

In some ways, what he had been through was worse than a war. And he survived it. He wasn't a hero, exactly, but he was a survivor. Surely his parents would invite him over for Sunday dinner. He imagined the whole family seated around a table filled with a platter of fried chicken and bowls of mashed potatoes and baskets of rolls. Then he would finally get a chance to wallow in what he still referred to as his "real home," even though he never had set foot in it.

In anticipation of that first dinner at his real home, Richard, while he was still at Coldwater, began asking around: How does a person go about finding another person's telephone number? At this point, he already had begun to develop a skill that would serve him well throughout his life, the ability to recognize people inclined to help him navigate the various mazes of modern society.

A large part of Richard's genius was an appreciation of his limitations. The fact that he couldn't read complicated his life considerably. He knew that there were some things he just couldn't figure out on his own. He devised a mechanism to compensate for his shortcomings, a highly sensitive, built-in Good Samaritan detector. Richard zeroed in on the wife of the man who ran the farm in Coldwater, as a woman who might help him. He was right. The woman showed Richard how to use directory assistance and helped him get the number of John and Dorothy Prangley in Grandville. He wrote it on a scrap of paper, tucked it into his wallet and smiled to himself, imagining the expressions on their faces when he placed his call. A telephone call from Richard! Wouldn't they be surprised!

By the time Richard walked out of Coldwater, he already had abandoned his plan to get settled in before placing the momentous telephone call. The fact is, he couldn't wait to get his hands on a phone and, in fact, would have prevailed upon the social worker driving the station wagon to stop at a telephone booth along the way, except that such a call would have violated the rules of Richard's "probation."

Residents on convalescent status were supposed to concentrate on the immediate business of living and working in the real world before they started thinking about reunions. Getting settled in was enough to worry about for the first few months. Besides, the goal was independence, not dependence on former arrangements that might no longer be functional. Reestablishing old ties was a longe-range goal, something to be attempted once the short-range goals had been accomplished.

But Richard set out for Pinerest with a solid plan and a pocketful of change. He could hardly sit still through his first stint on the job. Finally, it was break time, and while the other workers went for their cigarettes and coffee and pop, Richard bolted directly from his work station to a pay telephone he had staked out on the way in. He fed some coins into the telephone and dialed the number.

Dorothy Prangley answered. As Richard expected, she was surprised; shocked might be a better word. She knew, of course, that Richard was to be released from Coldwater and that he would be living in a group home in Grand Rapids. She and John had received a letter from Coldwater informing them of all that. But she surely hadn't expected to pick up the phone one day and hear somebody on the other end telling her he was Richard. She just wasn't ready for that. Dorothy asked Richard how he got their number. Richard took the question literally. He thought it meant that his mother was impressed with his ingenuity, but when he explained how he got the number, his mother didn't seem particularly awestruck.

Richard was fishing for an invitation. He was hoping his mother would ask him when he could come over for dinner. The conversation wasn't proceeding as it had in Richard's fantasy. His mother's tone wasn't ecstatic; it was cautious, almost apprehensive. Richard got the distinct impression that he was intruding. It sounded to him like his own mother was afraid of him. The invitation he had hoped for didn't come that day. It didn't come until much later. Richard went back to work that day with the familiar bitter taste in his mouth. His hopes had been so high. The disappointment settled into the pit of his stomach, where it remained for weeks.

Even then, Richard refused to abandon the fantasy he had been working on for 15 years, the fantasy that made him part of a real family. When the sophisticated approach didn't work, he tried others. He reasoned that perhaps once his parents actually *saw* that he was no longer the wild child, thrashing his way through life, they would want to be around him more. He called home every day and begged his parents to let him come to their home. Eventually, John and Dorothy Prangley invited their son to dinner, but not before they conducted an experiment, a dry run, so to speak, on neutral ground. The site they chose for the experiment was the woods near White Cloud, about 50 miles north of their home. They would take Richard on a family camping trip, just to see how things would go. Maybe, if Richard proved his behavior was under control and that he harbored no ill will against his parents, they could let him into their house.

Later that summer, John Prangley picked Richard up at the Hanson Home. Together they drove to the campsite, where they met Dorothy and some of Richard's siblings. It was an awkward, uncomfortable reunion, marked by a lot of politeness, but very little warmth. To his parents, Richard was a reminder of a part of their lives they wanted to forget. Obviously the people at Coldwater decided that Richard *was* capable of living outside the institution. Maybe the advice they received had been bad, and maybe they had too readily accepted it. Maybe they should have visited their son more and brought him home once in a while, at least at Christmas. Maybe they should have made a bigger effort to make him part of the family. These were troubling thoughts, and it was so much easier to bury them in more immediate concerns when Richard wasn't around.

To Richard's siblings, he was little more than an oddly behaving stranger with whom they happened to have blood ties. They were already a big family. By 1971, there were 10 Prangley offspring besides Richard. The eldest, was 27; the youngest

was an 11-year-old daughter, born four years after Richard took up residence at
Coldwater. To his youngest sister, Richard was little more than a rumor. It was
hard enough for the members of the sprawling Prangley brood to keep in touch
with their *close* relatives. It wasn't like they needed another sibling. Everybody tol-
erated the situation as best they could for two days. Since there were no disasters,
they planned another weekend in the woods, and another one after that.

Gradually, John and Dorothy Prangley came to see that Richard meant
them no harm. He was not an enraged victim looking for revenge; he was more
like a lost puppy looking for a pat on the head. He tended to rattle on a little
too much about how difficult life was inside the institution. But he seemed
essentially harmless. And it didn't seem likely he was going to go away. He wore
them down. After two months of intense lobbying by Richard, they relented.
They agreed to let their son into their home.

John Prangley retrieved his son at the Hanson Home on a Sunday afternoon in midsummer. Again, trying to show his parents and siblings he could fit
into society, that he was familiar with some of the rules, Richard had gone out
and bought a necktie. Knotting it around his collar that Sunday was a horrify-
ing experience for Richard. It took him back to that day in Cottage 41 when the
attendant grabbed his tie and nearly strangled him.

Slipping the knot higher, closing the loop tighter and tighter around his
neck, was almost more than Richard could bear. But he wanted to make a good
impression. If his father and brothers could wear neckties, so could he. If wearing a necktie was what it took to gain respect, he would do it. More than anything, Richard wanted to be like them. One way to be like them was to *look* like
them. He left the tie on.

Most of Richard's siblings were at their parents' home that day; some of
them still lived there. The dinner went reasonably well, but not exceptionally
so. Richard's dinner conversation left much to be desired. He couldn't talk
about family history, at least not the history anybody else wanted to discuss.
He didn't know what small talk was. Unfamiliar with the subtle art of tact,
Richard started with the questions again. Always the questions, and always
delivered so bluntly. With what must have seemed to John and Dorothy
Prangley like a perverse directness, their son would ask them, again and again,
why they sent him to Coldwater and why they left him there 15 years. Why
should they invite Richard into their home when they would be subjected to
third degree every time he came?

But Richard didn't ask the questions to torture his parents. And if there were
accusations implicit in his inquiries, they were unintentional. He just wanted
the truth. For 15 years, he had mulled the questions, never arriving any closer to
answers than when he had started. For 15 years, he had waited to ask them.
Finally he had a chance to pose his questions to the only people who could

answer them. He couldn't help himself. On his way to getting to know himself, to establishing his self-image, there were some things he needed to understand.

Gradually, Richard got answers to some of his questions. His parents described his premature birth and told him he was uncontrollable as a child, simply too much for them to handle. They decided to put him in Coldwater, they said, only after two doctors, a priest and a lot of other people who were experts in their field told them it would be the best thing for Richard. John and Dorothy Prangley told their son that, in those days, they didn't have any other options.

Richard had other questions. Why didn't his parents visit him more often when he was in the institution? And, finally, the question Richard pushed around, day after day, year after year, like a bucket of dirty water:

Why did they never take him home, not even at Christmas?

There were more questions, hundreds more. But Richard quickly figured something out. The more questions he asked about the old days, and the more he told his parents about the horrors of life inside the institution, the less they wanted him around.

They kept urging Richard to forget about the past and go on with his life. What was done, was done. He began to realize that if he wanted to get along with his parents, if he wanted to be let back into the family circle, he would have to keep his mouth shut about certain things. He tried it, on and off, with varying degrees of success. He tried to keep the past on a shelf in his closet. But when he least expected it, it would tumble down and break open, and the contents would spill out around his feet.

Some things, Richard couldn't change; some things, he could. A full month before Eunice wrote the letter outlining the difficulties he was having adjusting to his new life, Richard, chafing at the restrictions at the Hanson Home, had begun to lobby for full independence. His tireless single-mindedness on that score foreshadowed future campaigns in his life.

After nearly three months at the Hanson Home, Richard's complaints about life there were well documented. He didn't like being told when and what he could eat. Dinner at the Hanson Home was the same time for everybody. The fact that Richard couldn't get a hot meal when he returned home from work at 9 p.m. was a constant source of irritation for him. He didn't like having to negotiate whether his bedroom window should be opened or closed. He didn't like having no say in the decorating scheme. He didn't like the lack of privacy. He didn't like being separated from his possessions. He didn't like having his entertainment selected for him.

By then, he was getting to know some of the people he worked with at Butterworth Hospital. They talked about the things they did in their spare time, about the movies and restaurants they frequented. It sounded a lot better to Richard than visiting Mrs. Hanson's relatives.

It all boiled down to one thing: Richard didn't like the idea of not being completely free, of having to move in unison with the other residents of the Hanson Home. He was one balloon in a bunch, their strings held by one hand. What Richard had at the Hanson Home was a pretense of freedom. The more he saw of freedom, the more he wanted the genuine article. Richard yearned to be cut loose. He wanted to go his own way. In the end, the experts had admitted it — the 15 years in custodial care were inappropriate. As Richard saw it, his placement in the Hanson Home was also inappropriate. How much inappropriateness should one person have to take? He already had paid dearly for the mistakes of those who had underestimated him. Why should he continue to pay?

Richard was complaining. Was anybody listening? Richard didn't think so. He devised a mission for himself: to get the people in charge to pay attention. Then he came up with a plan.

On Aug. 8, Richard went to the Greyhound bus station in Grand Rapids and, using his developing knack for making people want to help him, got a ticket to Coldwater. He fully realized that leaving Grand Rapids without permission was a violation of the rules and he probably would get into hot water for it. But he was desperate. The people in charge at Coldwater could refuse to take his telephone calls. They could dismiss the complaints relayed to them by Eunice as the grumblings of a chronic malcontent. But if Richard showed up on their doorstep in person, they would have no choice but to give him some answers.

Richard's plan was to take his case to Gordon, the Coldwater social worker who seemed to be on his side. But Richard learned, through some telephone calls placed from the bus station in Coldwater, that Gordon had left the institution. Not knowing where else to turn, Richard boarded a bus back to Grand Rapids. That was merely one false start. Richard had no intention of giving up that easily. Determined to get his life started on his own terms, Richard returned to Coldwater three weeks later and succeeded in raising a ruckus. Writing for the record, another Coldwater social worker described the episode this way: "Aug. 28, 1971: At about 10:30 p.m. I received a telephone call from Richard at my home, stating that he had arrived in Coldwater earlier … and that he had come down to talk to the State Home staff about his unhappiness over his present placement at the [Hanson] Contract Home. I asked Richard if his caseworker in Grand Rapids knew that he had come to Coldwater. He said he hadn't told anyone, but that he was just so upset he had to make the trip. I reprimanded him for his lack of planning."

Richard assured the social worker that he had a place to sleep that night. He had planned to stay with a former Coldwater resident who had an apartment in town. But that plan fell through some time after 11 p.m. After the social worker got another call from Richard, he picked Richard up and drove him to several hotels. Unable to find a vacancy, Richard was driven to his former address, the

Coldwater State Home and Training School. Sticking to the rules, the staff members on duty that night said they could not accept a patient without a physical examination. The social worker arranged for one that night. Richard spent the weekend in Cottage 21.

On Monday, he was put on a bus back to Grand Rapids. Although he was going back to the Hanson Home, he had made his point and forced a discussion of his complaints. The records show a detailed examination of the situation in the days immediately following Richard's unauthorized appearance at Coldwater. Back in Grand Rapids, Richard's caseworker pointed out how well he was doing at work. For one thing, Eunice explained, Richard had nearly quadrupled his wages, from 50 cents an hour to $1.90 an hour, in three months.

Speculating on the motive for Richard's unauthorized visit to Coldwater, Eunice wrote: "Apparently Richard had been feuding with his roommate, over petty things, such as having windows opened or closed in their room. Richard continued to be angry because his boxes could not be stored in the room, while [his roommate] was allowed to have a bookcase there. It seems the room was changed around when new linoleum was laid. This was the last straw as far as Richard was concerned. No one had consulted him about the linoleum, or the new furniture arrangement.... The only subject Richard seems to talk about is his desire for independence from control and supervision."

No wonder. From Richard's point of view, it was the only thing *worth* talking about. It's what he had longed for and what he had expected. While lobbying to get out of the Hanson Home, Richard had been asking around, gathering information on various housing arrangements. Somebody at Butterworth told him about the YMCA, a place where a person could get a decent room without having to spend a fortune.

Within two months after his unauthorized trip to Coldwater, Richard was living at the YMCA in downtown Grand Rapids, a 15-minute walk from Butterworth Hospital. He also had a new caseworker, Brian, for reasons never explained to Richard.

In any case, Richard seemed to have better luck with the new caseworker. Somehow Richard convinced him that he could be happy, and less likely to create headaches, at the YMCA. Brian proposed the move to his supervisors "as a possible solution to [Richard's] living situation crisis." They bought it. Richard became a free man. The move from the Hanson Home officially released him, once and for all, from his connection to the Coldwater State Home and Training School. Richard's records were transferred from Coldwater to the State of Michigan Regional Mental Retardation Center in Muskegon, which served Kent County.

On His Own

In my room at the YMCA, I could play my music, I could watch TV late at night, I could put my stuff wherever I wanted to put it. I had my own key. I could come and go as I pleased. I didn't have to answer to nobody. Boy, that was a wonderful feeling.

— Richard Prangley

If the Hanson Home was purgatory, the YMCA was an unlikely heaven. This was the freedom for which Richard had been yearning. It wasn't much of a place: one room with a single bed, a closet and a chest of drawers. The bathroom was down the hall. But to Richard, it was a palace because it was his own place. He had the key. He controlled everything that went on within its four walls.

Employing careful organization, Richard managed to shoehorn all of his possessions into the room — the things he had brought from Coldwater and the things he had bought since arriving in Grand Rapids. In his own room, surrounded by his belongings, Richard was happier than he had ever been. He could play his 1950s rock 'n' roll music on his transistor radio without anybody telling him to turn it off. He could eat at the YMCA cafeteria or walk to the restaurant down the street whenever he felt like eating.

In fact, he could stay up until 2 a.m. eating strawberry pie and drinking coffee at the Big Boy if he wanted to. Well past midnight one memorable October night, Richard found himself doing just that, eating pie and drinking coffee at the Big Boy, and it occurred to him, in one big rush of satisfaction, that he was, indeed, a free man.

Since childhood, when he got into trouble for getting up in the middle of the night just to listen to the crickets chirp, Richard was a natural night owl, and his shift at the hospital let him indulge that impulse. Living at the YMCA, without having to answer to anybody, completed the package. There wasn't a single soul demanding to know where he was going and what time he would be home. There was nobody to restrain him in his bed.

Things got even better. Richard's room at the YMCA was one element short of perfection. It needed a TV, ideally a color TV. Richard started saving for it, but his rent at YMCA was higher than it had been at the Hanson Home. And the food in the real world was so tempting and expensive. Clearly, it would be a long time before he'd be able to save enough for a color TV. But one of Richard's friends at Butterworth told him about buying things on credit, paying for them a little at a time, but getting them right away. Richard had a steady job. His expenses were modest. Maybe he could qualify for credit.

Fox Jewelers in downtown Grand Rapids took a chance on Richard. He spent what amounted to a month's pay on a brand-new color TV. They even delivered it to his room at the YMCA. He would pay it off month by month. Richard had established credit and he had his own color TV in his own room. He could watch whatever channel he wanted, whenever he wanted — first thing in the morning and late into the night. He could turn the TV off when he got tired of it. He could take it with him when he moved. It was his color TV.

Life was good, so good, in fact, that Richard knew he couldn't have accomplished what he had without some help from his most powerful ally, whom he referred to as "the Man upstairs." While Richard was living at the group home, Mrs. Hanson, a devout Catholic, was more than willing to keep Richard on the correct spiritual path. She took Richard to services at her church, St. Alphonsus. It was Richard's first experience with a real church, and he was dazzled, not only by the pomp and ceremony of the services, but by the beauty of the church itself.

Something came over him when the organ started and the voices of the congregation rose in unison, a soothing, peaceful feeling. The people there, naturally on their best behavior, treated him so well. They didn't seem to notice his shortcomings. Or, if they did, they didn't let on. In church, the fact that Richard was a little different didn't seem to matter. Everybody told him that, in God's eyes, all people are equal, regardless of whether they are slow learners, or whether they had spent 15 years inside an institution.

This definitely was something Richard wanted to get involved in. Out from under Mrs. Hanson's wing, Richard continued to nurture his spiritual impulses. While living at the YMCA, he started regularly attending St. Andrew's Catholic Cathedral, a church within easy walking distance of the "Y."

Meanwhile, the move to the YMCA was so successful that on June 1, 1972, Richard's caseworker, Brian, suggested that the strings between Richard and the state mental health system be cut altogether. Richard had been living at the YMCA for two years. He was ready to move on. He wanted his own bathroom. Brian wrote:

It is our hope and our goal that the young people released from your center make the best possible adjustment to the community living and becoming meaningful citizens with purpose in their life and goals to strive for. It is precisely this situation which Richard Prangley has achieved.

As you probably remember, about nine months ago Richard encountered a few problems while living at the [Hanson] Home. Rather than have him returned to the center, we moved him into the YMCA, hoping that more freedom and less structure was the type of environment he needed. As it turned out, the choice was a good one. In these past months, Richard has not had any serious problems and his adjustment is more than satisfactory. He has made friends at the YMCA, and the director has mentioned to me several times that he is a good tenant and there have been no complaints against him. He has many possessions and these are always well taken care of. Each item has its own place in his room, and although overcrowded, the room is always neat and clean.

Richard's employment record is excellent, and his supervisors have nothing but praise for him. In these past several months, he has made several trips on his own and they were successful. He is now almost completely independent and is paying his own way for everything. He has purchased a new color TV and has made the payments without difficulty, and still he has managed to save over $300.

Because Richard has made such good progress, I felt he was ready to be more independent. He was given permission to rent an apartment of his own and he is moving in this week.... Because of his progress and his excellent adjustment to the community, I believe he is ready to be discharged from convalescent status.

He ... has set many goals for himself. Among them are: to have his rights reinstated, to find a better job (perhaps as a carpenter), to buy his own home and to be totally independent. He has achieved much, is happy and enjoys life. With adequate support and guidance he will in the near future become independent. This day will become reality soon and it is this kind of success we hope to have with everyone.

On June 7, 1972, one year and 21 days after Richard walked out of Coldwater, an interdepartmental note went from Jim Powers, medical records supervisor of the Mental Retardation Center in Muskegon, to Dr. Cornwell: "Attached is a request by Brian ... for the discharge of Richard Prangley, age 23, from convalescent status.... From what Brian has told me, Richard has a tremendous drive for independence and has made significant steps in this direction. He is currently living in an apartment, steadily employed and fully self-supporting.... May we have your approval for his unconditional release?"

Dr. Cornwell scrawled at the bottom of the same page: "Okay, above discharge approved."

Five days later the discharge was executed. Richard was free. Officially, anyway. Of course, slipping the bonds of 15 years of custodial care would require more than a doctor's signature. In later years, the experts would say that Richard's biggest handicap was the loss of 15 years, 15 *crucial* years, of nor-

mal socialization. The absence of academic training in Richard's life, as cata-
strophic as it was, was only part of what he had lost. During the years when
most people learn the important lessons about how to function in society,
Richard was virtually living in a cave. He would never be able to completely
undo that, but he would never stop trying.

There was one more step in the official extrication. Two weeks later, Richard
petitioned the Kent County Probate Court to change his status in the eyes of
the law. The hearing was scheduled for July 10. Richard, his father and Brian tes-
tified in open court. After listening to the testimony and reviewing Richard's
records, the Honorable Richard N. Loughrin wrote: "It is ordered, adjudged
and decreed that Richard Leigh Prangley is not now mentally handicapped."

In the eyes of the law, Coldwater State Home and Training Center had done
its job. Richard had been cured.

By the summer of 1972, barely a year after he walked out of the Coldwater
institution, Richard had progressed through the Hanson Home, two rooms at
the YMCA and finally had landed in his first real apartment, the lower flat of a
house. And it was within walking distance of Butterworth. He had five rooms
all to himself, a bedroom, a kitchen, a living room, a dining room, and a bathroom — his own bathroom. He also had a place to prepare his own meals. To
Richard, the space was enormous.

The apartment was only partially furnished, and Richard's head spun with
thoughts of filling those five rooms. He bought a stereo system to go with his
TV. He bought dishes, pots and pans. He got into the habit of frying steaks in a
skillet and baking pies — not bad for a "low-grade imbecile."

Richard remained in the same job at Butterworth and was still earning $1.90
an hour. But his expenses also remained modest. He didn't own a car and did-
n't even have to spend bus fare to get to work. Being able to prepare his own
meals allowed him to cut down on his restaurant expenses. Richard experi-
mented with other ways to cut his costs. Some, like packing a lunch to take to
work, succeeded. Others, like taking in borders, nearly ruined him.

It wasn't strictly economics that inspired Richard to take in some former
Coldwater residents who had gone the same route he had — from the institution, to a group home, to independent living — but without the same success.
As an advocate, Richard felt inclined to practice what he preached. At one point,
three former Coldwater residents were sharing his house. Much to Richard's
frustration and disappointment, the arrangement collapsed. Eventually, Richard
became the only one contributing toward household expenses. Ultimately,
Richard showed his three roommates the door.

Richard survived that setback. After two years in the house, he was ready
for something better yet. He moved his growing pile of possessions into a mod-

ern apartment complex. Now Richard had everything he ever wanted, plus a dishwasher and air-conditioning, too.

Richard's appetites got bigger. His tastes became more expensive. His freedom started getting the better of him as his urge to acquire more and more possessions started overtaking his resources. One of his friends at Butterworth told him about "plastic cash," a card that a person could use "just like money," a phrase Richard took too literally.

On the strength of a steady job and a brief, but unblemished, credit history, Richard soon had a credit card. He bought a second television, a large console model. He put the first TV in his living room and put the smaller one in his bedroom. He bought a bigger and better stereo. It was easy. All he had to do was show his card and sign his name. He could have anything he wanted.

Richard had a vague idea that at some point he would have to pay for all of it with the money he brought home from Butterworth, but he was assured by the sales people that the monthly payments would be affordable. Individually, they were. But as a total package, they were too much.

Richard's reading skills were rudimentary at best. When the blizzard of mail started coming, he gathered it up and took it to work with him. One of his coworkers sorted it out and informed Richard that his monthly bills exceeded his monthly income. That was the bottom line. Richard's solution was to take a second job. Anything would be better than having to part with his beloved possessions.

Richard went to work bussing tables and washing dishes at the Knife and Fork Restaurant at the Pantlind Hotel in downtown Grand Rapids. By then, he was working the day shift at Butterworth, having transferred from the kitchen to maintenance, where he worked on the hospital's grounds. Four days a week, he would go directly from an eight-hour shift at the hospital to an eight-hour shift at the restaurant. His workday went from 7 a.m. until midnight.

It was during this period that Richard experienced a rare attempt at brotherly love. One of Richard's brothers, the one who had been born just 8 ½ months before Richard's premature entry into the world, decided he would teach Richard how to read. Once or twice a week, he would come to Richard's apartment. The two brothers would sit at the dining room table, and, using flash cards and other materials, Richard's brother would attempt to help him unlock the secrets of the written language.

Although Richard appreciated the attempt, the sessions did not go particularly well. Richard's brother had no experience teaching the mentally impaired. And although Richard was eager to reward his brother's efforts, most of the time he was utterly baffled by the concepts presented to him. It was a frustrating experience for both men, particularly Richard. He went along, hoping that at some point a light would go on inside his head and he would finally be able to grasp what his brother was offering him. But the switch never clicked, and gradually the sessions came to an end.

As if Richard didn't have enough going in his life at the time, he was about to become a movie star. A group of filmmakers from Detroit became interested in Richard's story. They called themselves the Detroit Film Collective and formed a nonprofit corporation in 1972. In its literature, the Collective described itself as a "group of people experienced in different areas of media [dedicated to] utilizing media as a tool for creating humane communication."

The Collective was 1970s idealism to the core: "As people, we must understand each other and our environment to survive, love and grow together. To understand, we must rely on communication which reflects a real awareness of people and our planet. Humane communications created with understanding and empathy can help people survive, love and grow."

The Detroit Film Collective was working on a documentary about people with mental disabilities titled *Readin' and Writin' Ain't Everything*. Coming from a definite anti-institution perspective, the goal of the film was to portray the mentally retarded as genuine human beings, capable of living worthwhile lives in the world at large and contributing to society.

The brochure promoting the film put it this way:

> Dispelling the myth that retarded people are incapable of living in the community, this film illustrates the positive efforts by retarded persons, their families and their communities to provide a variety of programs which facilitate maximum human growth.
>
> The uniqueness of each situation depicted in the film further illustrates the individuality of each person with mental retardation and the need for community programs that meet individual needs, regardless of intellectual capacity.

The idea was no-frills real-life-as-art. The filmmakers focused on four people who exemplified the concept of mainstreaming and showed straightforward slices of their lives. Apparently the Collective got Richard's name from the Kent County Consultation Center, the agency that had monitored Richard's return to society from Coldwater. Richard became one of the stars of the 26-minute movie and, again displayed his knack for coming up with the right phrase at the right time, apparently contributed the movie's title.

In the promotional pamphlet, Richard is quoted as saying: "When I got out and went to Grand Rapids, I felt like a million-dollar man. That's what living on your own's all about: having your freedom. Maybe I can't read or write, but I can still make a go of living in this world, and readin' and writin' ain't everything as long as you put your head to it."

The film opens with the mournful wailing of a solo harmonica and bleak footage of the Coldwater grounds. The camera lingers on a sign that says, "No Trespassing, State Property," then pans along the red brick buildings. It shows some residents shuffling around in the courtyard, then goes inside one of the dayrooms and shows residents lined up on the wooden benches. One boy is contorted on the floor; another boy rocks back and forth.

Richard's voice starts:

> They said I was having a little problem going to school in the outside community because I couldn't do anything. Then some doctor my parents met told them where to send me. So my parents got a court order and got permission to send me away there.
>
> The first place I went to was Cottage 41. I was there most of my life. I didn't have it so good down there. I didn't have a chance to get the schooling I needed. I was locked up in a ward all the time down there. We called it the funny farm. Most of us kids called it the funny farm. The farm where we were caged in like animals. Too many people were locked in dayrooms like animals. It was like being in a zoo; that's the life I went through. That's why I ran away so many times. I didn't believe in being locked in. If the attendants did something bad to you and you tell the head boss over them ... If they find out, they really work you over, beat up on you so you don't do it again.
>
> My parents would come up to see me around Christmastime. Sometimes they'd come up in the summer and take me on a picnic. Some years they didn't come up at all. I wanted to go home and I never could. I never went home at all. While I lived there, I never went home. It's some life you go through when you're retarded.

The film then shows Richard sitting on the concrete steps of Cottage 21, where he lived immediately prior to his release. He talks about getting out of Coldwater and going to Grand Rapids. He talks about the joys of being independent.

The film then follows Richard through his routine at Butterworth, punching the time clock, rounding up his cleaning supplies and going to work mopping a floor. It shows him relaxing in front of the television in his tidy apartment. His voice loosely narrates the scene: "I've got an apartment in Grand Rapids and got it fixed up nice. I've got all the privacy I need. I like to live nice and clean and try to make the best of my life in this world."

The camera then follows Richard to his job at the restaurant and shows him in a white uniform, bussing tables and interacting with his coworkers. In his voiceover, he talks about what he does at the restaurant and why he needs a second job. "I've got two jobs because I need a little more money for some bills I have to pay.... I'm learning every day, every month, every year. I might be able to have my own house in the near future."

As portrayed in *Readin' and Writin' Ain't Everything*, Richard's life appeared to be on a steady rise. He was out of the institution. He was making a go of it out in the world. He was, indeed, a fine example of a person proving that a mental handicap didn't necessarily preclude a productive, fulfilling life. In reality, the plot was about to take a radical twist. Off the screen, Richard was on the verge of his first major setback since leaving the institution.

A Step Backward

I heard Mom and Dad talking. I thought they were saying that maybe I shouldn't be living on my own — that I wasn't ready. I didn't know for sure they were saying that, but I didn't want to take any chances. I wasn't going back to no group home. I got out of there.

— Richard Prangley

Working two jobs and reining in his impulse to acquire more and more material possessions, Richard was keeping his head above water. In 1975, an opportunity to further cut expenses came by way of an offer from one of Richard's coworkers at Butterworth, a parking ramp attendant.

The attendant, a recovering alcoholic, rented a house not far from the hospital. He proposed that Richard move in with him. The two could share expenses and Richard could cut his housing expenses considerably. What's more, there was a spare room in the back of the house that Richard could use for the workshop he always wanted. Richard accepted the offer and moved his belongings into the house.

An expert in grounds maintenance — it was part of his job at Butterworth, after all — Richard assumed responsibility for cutting the lawn, raking leaves, shoveling snow and all the other outside chores. He enjoyed the work but lacked the tools to do a thorough, professional job. Butterworth had the right tools, everything he needed. Richard got permission from his immediate supervisor to borrow the tools and began taking them home regularly.

Meanwhile, Richard had been taking home other things from Butterworth, cabinets and other small pieces of furniture that were damaged or no longer needed. They were things the hospital was about to throw away. Richard liked to repair the discards in his workshop, then use them or give them to his friends. But he never took anything home without permission. While it was true that his moral training had been sporadic at best, he certainly knew what stealing was. It was wrong. And it could land him in another institution. That thought alone was more than enough to keep Richard honest for the rest of his life.

About eight months after Richard moved in, he returned home from a weekend trip to find that the lock on one of his workshop cabinets had been broken. An electric drill was missing. Richard confronted his roommate, who claimed to know nothing about the theft. Richard didn't buy that. He believed it was either he who had stolen the drill, or one of his friends. Richard was certain of that. The two men argued. Richard's roommate stuck to his story that he knew nothing about the theft. Richard felt betrayed.

A few days later, the Grand Rapids police arrived at Richard's house with a search warrant. Assisted by Butterworth officials, they rounded up the yard tools that belonged to the hospital and made note of the fact that some other things that had once been hospital property also were found in the apartment.

His roommate, it seemed, had turned Richard in.

Richard heard his Miranda rights, which he didn't understand at all. He was fingerprinted. His mug shot was taken. His parents had to post bail to keep him out of jail. Apparently, the people who had given Richard permission to take the items of furniture and borrow the yard tools had done so on their own, and this, apparently, was a violation of hospital policy. To save their own jobs, they denied authorizing Richard's actions. It was their word against the word of a man who had spent 15 years inside an institution.

Hospital officials gave Richard a choice: Resign, or face felony charges. Richard quit. His five-year career at Butterworth was over.

After posting bail for Richard, John and Dorothy Prangley took their son to their house in Grandville. Later, his brother helped him move his belongings into the basement of the Prangley house.

It was a supreme irony: After 20 years of yearning for it, Richard finally was sleeping in his parents' home. And he was thoroughly miserable. He had come home a failure. He felt like an intruder, an obstacle that everybody else in the house had to step around. He could see it in their eyes: They believed that, despite all his high-flying talk about everything he had accomplished since leaving the institution, he ultimately had failed in his attempt to live independently.

Richard didn't know how much of his story his parents believed. In any case, he couldn't dispute the fact that he barely had escaped felony charges. And here he was, jobless and homeless. His parents and siblings sized up the piles of Richard's belongs and shook their head.

They asked him why he didn't have more self-control. Did he have to buy everything he saw?

What's more, he wouldn't stop talking about how tough he had it inside the institution. There he went again, blaming all of his troubles on Coldwater and, by implication, the people who put him there. Before long, he started with all his bothersome questions again.

Obviously, things couldn't go on the way they were. But what were John and Dorothy Prangley to do with Richard? They didn't have any legal responsibility for him; Richard was a grown man, on his own. And wasn't that exactly what he wanted? Wasn't he constantly harping about his precious independence? On the other hand, they couldn't just turn him out on the streets.

Maybe, John and Dorothy Prangley surmised, Richard wasn't quite ready for full-blown freedom. Maybe everybody acted too hastily in moving him out of the Hanson Home. Richard began picking up snatches of hushed conversations. He began to get a bad feeling, a feeling that his parents were considering another group home. The mere thought of it made Richard nauseous. He had come too far. He could never go back to a place where people told him how to live. Sure, he had made some poor decisions and had run into a streak of bad luck, but that was life on the outside. He had enjoyed some successes, too. This was just a temporary setback. He would get back on track.

Richard spent two weeks in his "real home" only to discover that it wasn't his real home after all. Without knowing it, Richard had crossed a line. Maybe it happened the day he walked out of Coldwater. Maybe it happened when he moved into the YMCA. In any case, Richard was no longer willing to leave his fate in the hands of others. He would succeed or fail on his own.

One night, Richard packed a suitcase. He got up very early the next morning and, without saying good-bye to his parents or siblings, he left his parents' house. Outside, he caught a taxi and told the driver to take him to the Greyhound bus station, where he bought a ticket to Detroit.

During the filming of *Readin' and Writin' Ain't Everything,* the people from the Detroit Film Collective took a liking to Richard. After the project was finished and they were saying their good-byes, the filmmakers told Richard that if he ever found himself in a jam, he should look them up. It seemed like a perfect time to take them up on their offer.

Richard had been a frequent weekend visitor to Detroit during the filming of *Readin' and Writin' Ain't Everything.* During those trips, he had learned a little about the city and how it was arranged. He arrived at the Greyhound bus station in Detroit in midmorning. From there, he took a city bus down Woodward Avenue to the apartment of one of the filmmakers, a man named Clyde.

All the members of the Film Collective had taken Richard under their wings during the production. Clyde, in particular, told Richard from time to time that if he ever needed a place to crash, there would always be a bed and a hot meal for him in Detroit.

Out of the blue, Richard knocked on Clyde's door the morning he fled Grandville. Clyde made good on his offer. Richard used Clyde's telephone to call Grandville and tell his parents that he was in Detroit, safe and sound, embarking on a new life.

Richard spent six months in Detroit, living with the various members of the Film Collective, staying a few weeks in one apartment, a few weeks in another apartment. It was a period of retreat for Richard, a time to lick his wounds, take stock of life outside the institution and consider his future prospects.

Even in that state of retrenchment, Richard continued to enjoy small advances on his journey toward an independent life. For one thing, he landed a job without the help of anybody. It was the first time in his life he had done so. One morning, Richard simply walked into the Fisher Building and asked around until he found the man responsible for hiring the building's cafeteria crew. Richard leveled with the man. He told him he wasn't able to fill out an application, but that he would answer any questions the man might have, and he would answer them honestly. He told the man where he had been and what he had done. The man put Richard to work washing dishes and bussing tables in the building's cafeteria.

The Film Collective people were generous hosts, and they made good on their promise to provide Richard shelter if he ever happened to find himself out on the street, but their lifestyle was not Richard's. For one thing, they frequently smoked marijuana. It seemed to Richard that they were always sitting around twisting the ends of their roll-your-own cigarettes, or passing their pipes to each other, while jazz oozed from the stereo.

The music was keeping Richard up at night. The smoke was bothering his sinuses. Richard began to get the feeling he was living in a cloud. Soon he developed a profound need for fresh air, both literally and figuratively. After six weeks of spinning his wheels, Richard decided it was time to get serious about getting back on track. And the first thing he had to do, he concluded, was leave Detroit.

Richard stretched his feelers toward Ypsilanti, a town about 40 miles southwest of Detroit. He had kept in touch, off and on, with Andy (not his real name), a former staff member from Coldwater, the same staff member, in fact, who had been Richard's host on all those working vacations in his final years in the institution. After leaving Coldwater, Andy went to work in the forensic center at the state hospital. He invited Richard to Ypsilanti, telling him that perhaps there was a job for him at the hospital.

With no better offers on the table, Richard accepted. He moved into the basement of the house in the nearby town of Petersburg, where Andy lived with his wife and three children. While waiting for an opening at the state hospital, Richard took a job at the Holiday Inn in Toledo, Ohio, riding a bus every morning across the state line. After three or four months, Andy got Richard a job in the hospital's kitchen, doing janitorial work and unloading trucks. Richard rode with Andy to and from work every day.

It was a convenient arrangement, but the convenience came at an exorbitant price: Richard's independence. Richard liked living in a family atmosphere and he appreciated the fact that Andy and his wife were trying to help him get his life straightened out. After the trouble in Grand Rapids and the wheel-spinning in Detroit, Richard felt he definitely needed some order and direction in his life. Still, it was a stifling existence compared to his life in Grand Rapids and Detroit. Not only was he dependent on Andy for his job, his food, his shelter and his transportation, but he was also forced to beg for spending money.

Every two weeks, Richard turned his paycheck over to Andy, and Andy gave him $20 or so for pocket money. The rest of it, Andy told Richard, covered his room and board. Even though Richard's command of mathematics was no more than rudimentary, he had the uneasy feeling that it didn't add up. To make matters worse, something depressingly familiar started happening. Richard's share of the household chores grew bigger and bigger, while everybody else's grew smaller. Again, he was doing all the dirty work.

While he was at Coldwater, the "working vacations" supposedly were educational. Theoretically, anyway, they were teaching him how to stay on task until a job was finished. They were preparing him for life on the outside. The arrangement at Andy's house was something else. Richard wasn't learning a thing scrubbing floors in Ypsilanti. He already knew more than he needed to know about scrubbing and polishing and mowing.

Richard felt like a slave. He worked all day at the hospital, then worked when he got home at night. On weekends, he worked some more. He was paying his way, and then some. Why should he have to work so much?

It so happened he wasn't getting good advice, either. Richard still had unsettled debts in Grand Rapids, but, under Andy's guidance, he bought a bedroom suite and other furniture on credit. The new purchases only added to the financial tangle that eventually would trip Richard.

And, finally, there was Andy's annoying habit. He liked to hit Richard. Richard never knew when Andy might walk up and start using him as punching bag. Andy kept saying he was just playing around, and at first it seemed that he was. But as time went on, it began to feel less like horseplay and more like something else. Sometimes Andy got carried away. Increasingly, his punches hurt more and more. Richard didn't like it; he had been punched enough in Coldwater to last the rest of his life.

After eight months of trading self-determination for security, Richard grew weary of the deal. He decided once again to take control of his life. No amount of security, he told himself, was worth the loss of independence he was experiencing at Andy's house. It was just too high a price to pay. Even the YMCA in Grand Rapids was better than this; a lot better, as a matter of fact. After weeks of brooding about it, Richard finally worked up the nerve to tell Andy what he thought of the arrangement. A big argument ensued. Richard moved his belongings to an apartment. The problem was that the state hospital was miles from Ypsilanti's business district.

The closest apartment he could afford was two miles from his job. There was no public transportation, and, being on the outs with Andy, Richard's only option was to walk two miles to the hospital and two miles home, every day. Luckily, it was summer. But that wasn't the only problem. Not only was Richard two miles from his job, he was even more isolated from stores and restaurants and movie theaters. He was forced to depend on rides from friends just to buy groceries. It was not a good arrangement. After four months of walking two miles to work and begging for rides, Richard decided that his life in Ypsilanti had run its course. Winter was coming and those walks to work soon would be more than just a nuisance.

Beyond that, the need to make a fresh run at independence was keeping Richard up at night. His life since he left Grand Rapids hadn't been the real thing, at least not the way he had envisioned it. His life in Grand Rapids had been the real thing. In Grand Rapids, working at Butterworth Hospital and living in an apartment with easy access to everything he needed, Richard had gotten a taste of how life should be. Detroit was an escape, a place for Richard to catch his breath and make a plan. Ypsilanti had been a step backward, a quest for security, a retreat into the familiar.

Now, Richard was looking to pick up the trail of the new life he sought. He had to make a decision. He didn't want to go back to Detroit. He couldn't go back to Grand Rapids. He had pretty much burned his bridges, at least for the time being, with his parents in Grandville. Richard was looking for a new start. Not just another apartment and another janitorial job in another Michigan town, but a fresh beginning. Richard believed he was at a crossroads. In his long walks to and from work every day in the late summer of 1977, Richard considered and reconsidered his options. He came up with a radical answer. He did what so many other Americans looking for a fresh start have done since the Gold Rush; he went west to California.

Why California? Why not? Richard wanted something that wasn't Michigan, and California certainly wasn't Michigan. It was far away from Michigan; so far away, in fact, that the people in California didn't even know that Richard Prangley had spent 15 years in an institution. They didn't know Richard's own parents put him there when he was only six. They didn't know that those same parents never took him home again. They didn't know he had been sexually abused in that institution. They didn't know Richard had gotten himself into financial trouble and that he had been forced to resign from his job. The people in California didn't know doctors had once declared Richard an imbecile who was incapable of learning anything.

Besides, Richard had heard what everybody said about California. It was where people went when they wanted to start over. He saw a movie about it once. California was the land of second chances, and a second chance was exactly what he needed. To Richard, it sounded like the perfect place for him.

Richard went to the municipal airport in Ypsilanti and bought an airline ticket. Then he sold as many of his possessions as he could, including the new bedroom suite he hadn't paid for yet. He sold the suite to his landlord. What he couldn't sell, he put into storage.

In late September, as winter was creeping up on Ypsilanti, Richard left town with a suitcase full of clothes and about $3,000 cash in his wallet. He took a bus from Ypsilanti to Detroit Metropolitan Airport. He couldn't read what his ticket said. He didn't know where he should go to catch his plane or what to do with his luggage. He just did what he always did in that situation. He approached one stranger after another until he found one willing to help a person whose speech and mannerisms weren't quite normal. Then Richard would pump that person for all the information he had. If it wasn't everything Richard needed, he moved on to the next person willing to make eye contact with him. Richard was like a panhandler, except that it wasn't loose change he sought, it was useful facts.

Some of the people Richard approached simply failed to meet his gaze. Some altered their course to avoid the man with the institutional shuffle, the halting, short-stepped gait that Richard would keep for the rest of his life. Also, Richard had the unnerving habit of refusing to meet the eyes of the people he spoke to. It was another residual of life inside the institution. It was another defense mechanism; looking somebody in the eyes was too risky. It made a person too vulnerable.

Some of the people Richard approached recoiled from him, as though they thought he was about to attack them. Often, it took him a long time to find somebody willing to stop long enough to listen to his questions and respond to them. When he found the right person — in Richard's view, God always seemed to make sure one appeared eventually — he asked the necessary questions; he got pointed in the right direction. And so it went at Metro Airport. At about 5 p.m., having asked the right questions of the right people, Richard climbed aboard an airplane for the first time in his life. He had a ticket to L.A. One way.

As the plane lifted from the runway, Richard watched the houses and fields of Wayne County recede in the September drizzle. Ypsilanti was down there, somewhere. So was Detroit and Grand Rapids and Grandville. So was the Coldwater State Home and Training School. The Hanson Home. The YMCA. Butterworth Hospital. Richard was leaving all those things.

He was leaving his whole life. He was going to a place where it was summer all year long. Maybe he would come back to Michigan someday for a visit. Maybe, after he got settled in Los Angeles, after he got a job and a nice apartment, he would call his parents and invite them out to California, where they could swim in the ocean any time of year. Richard would take them on a tour. Wouldn't *that* knock them for a loop? Richard making a go of it in California, with the movie stars — making something of himself, after all. Surely they would love and respect him after that.

Even at the airport in Los Angeles, Richard found somebody willing to take the time to answer his questions and get him headed in the right direction. He managed to find his suitcase and the airport bus that would take him into downtown L.A. The people who took the time to answer Richard's questions kept asking him the same thing: At which hotel did he have a reservation? He wasn't quite sure what they meant by that. He climbed on the bus and asked the driver to let him know when he was downtown. The driver, accustomed to eccentric, confused passengers, stopped the bus at some point and told Richard it was his stop.

Dressed in his customary flannel shirt and baggy jeans, Richard stepped off the bus, into the warm L.A. night, and walked into the first hotel he saw. It happened to be the Boniventure. Richard asked the clerk how much it would cost to stay there and was shocked by what the clerk told him. At that rate, he wouldn't last a week in L.A., even if he didn't eat anything. And it might take him longer than a week to get a job. He checked in at a nearby Holiday Inn.

For six days, Richard walked around the city, applying for jobs at restaurants, hotels — wherever somebody was willing to take his name and his telephone number at the hotel. He even took a taxi to the State of California civil service office and got somebody there to help him fill out an application. The rest of the time, he wandered around L.A., taking in the sights — the shops and restaurants, the traffic, the endless streams of people, all colors and shapes, and all of them in a hurry except the panhandlers and the dispossessed, sitting on sidewalks and sleeping in lobbies.

There was plenty to see. Often Richard would stop somebody and start asking his questions and the person would start speaking another language. This frightened Richard. What if he really needed help one day and the only person around couldn't speak English? One night, having lost his bearings in the wrong part of town, he became so frustrated that he admonished one man on the street to "talk English." The man took offense and nearly attacked Richard.

Unable to read or write, Richard survived in unfamiliar environments by asking questions. It was the way he compensated for his inability to read. It was necessary for him to live in a place where he could get his questions answered — in English. His hostile encounter with the non-English-speaking man on the street convinced him that maybe L.A. wasn't for him, after all. Maybe, when it came right down to it, he was a Michigan person.

Seven days after he arrived in California, having no job offers and $2,000 less than when he arrived, Richard bought a one-way ticket back to Michigan. This time, he picked an unlikely destination, an improbable setting for his rebirth: Coldwater.

Ironic? Maybe so. The choice, however, was not without a certain logic. Richard knew the lay of the land in Coldwater. He also knew people there. Many of the residents who left the institution settled in Coldwater simply because that's where they found themselves and because they had no compelling reasons to go anywhere else. And much of the Coldwater staff lived there, too.

In Ypsilanti, Richard had been isolated. In L.A., he may as well have been on another planet. Maybe what he needed, after all, was some familiar surroundings. Maybe, he figured, he could get a job at the institution. The place was, of course, a mountain of bad memories. But working there would be a lot better than living there. And just maybe he would be able to help change things. He knew, as well as anybody, what changes were needed.

A job at the institution never materialized. Richard spent his first two months in Coldwater living in the Rescue Mission, a shelter for the homeless. Social Services set him up with general assistance, a subsistence-level stipend paid to unemployable adults, and eventually found him a part-time janitorial job at the Army recruiting station in town. It was a temporary setback. As he always had done, Richard began climbing out of the pit almost as soon as he landed in it.

He met a man who worked at the Essex Plastic and Metal factory in town. The man turned out to be one of the many people who seemed to appear at crucial points in Richard's life, the people Richard referred to as "guardian angels." The man got Richard a maintenance job at Essex. Richard went to work. He went off general assistance. He moved from the Rescue Mission to a modest one-room flat. He quickly settled into a routine.

Every working day, he rose at dawn, jumped into the communal shower before the other tenants got to it, then walked to a doughnut shop, where he ate a couple of jelly doughnuts — three on some days — and drank two cups of coffee. His supervisor at Essex drove by the doughnut shop on his way to the plant, picked up Richard and transported him the five miles to the factory.

At Essex, Richard was responsible for cleaning and maintaining the cafeteria, offices and hallways. He ordered his own supplies. Richard quickly earned a reputation as a good worker. He was somebody who would stick with a job until it was done and sometimes show initiative. In the cafeteria, Richard took it upon himself to repaint the walls, tables and trash barrels, replacing the drab colors with bright ones. He was well liked, too. And while his fellow workers kept pictures of their kids on the inside of the doors of their lockers, Richard kept a small American flag and a picture of Jesus.

One of his coworkers noticed the photo one day and asked Richard about his religious beliefs. Richard told the man that he believed, first and foremost that "the Man upstairs" was watching out for him and had, in fact, bailed him out of many tight spots. The man was active in the Coldwater Church of Christ. He invited Richard to a Sunday service. It was good timing. It just so happened that Richard was, at the time, without an official religious affiliation. He had drifted away from the Catholic church during his trouble in Grand Rapids and the bouncing around that followed.

In truth, it wasn't simply a lack of stability and opportunity. There was more to it — a true disenchantment with Catholicism. Richard had begun to take issue with some of the practices of Catholics, primarily their tolerance of gambling and especially their tolerance of gambling right in church buildings. He knew people who went to bingo games in the same buildings where they worshipped. Somewhere along the way, he had seen a movie about the life of Jesus Christ in which an angry Christ tipped over the table of a group of gamblers. For reasons Richard could never quite explain, the scene made a big impression on him.

Still, Richard missed that soothing, peaceful feeling that used to comfort him, like a warm bath, whenever he went to church. He missed the singing and the sense of community. Also, he was convinced that "the Man upstairs" was looking out for him, and Richard had not been particularly good about showing his gratitude. He was eager to get reconnected spiritually.

Also, he was eager to start making some friends, real friends. Richard began to notice that while he got along well with people and he had many casual acquaintances, he wasn't doing much socializing, not in the conventional sense. People frequently expressed admiration for what Richard had managed to overcome and what he stood for, but they tended to go only so far with him. They didn't often invite him to their houses or make plans to go out with him to restaurants or movies.

Richard immediately liked the Church of Christ. The services were so much livelier than the Catholic services. The people were outgoing. And it wasn't a Sunday-only religion. There seemed to be something going on all the time. Richard liked it so much he decided to be baptized into the church. Dressed in a robe, he stepped up to the altar one day and settled into a large vat of water while the minister prayed over him. He asked Jesus for forgiveness. He cried genuine tears.

Now that Richard had tended to his spiritual affairs, there was another, more earthly matter that demanded his attention. Something had been looming over him, threatening to derail him all over again. The haunting truth was that Richard had never settled his debts. He still owed money in Grand Rapids and Ypsilanti. The bills hadn't caught up with him yet in Coldwater. Maybe they never would. But he didn't want to take that chance.

Heading out to the coast, Richard had almost managed to convince himself he could run away from the bills. Deep inside, he knew running was not a responsible way to conduct his affairs, nor was it what "the Man upstairs" would want him to do. Beyond that, it probably wouldn't work anyway. If he was ever going to prove the "experts" wrong, the ones who said he was incapable of life on the outside, he would have to own up to his responsibilities. He didn't want to live with the feeling that something was sneaking up on him, ready to pounce.

What if he got into trouble over it? What if somebody tried to use it as proof that Richard wasn't equipped to live independently, after all? He heard somewhere that sometimes people went to prison for not paying their bills. He sure didn't need that hanging over his head. Again, Richard started asking questions. How would he go about settling the score? The questions led to a lawyer in Coldwater. The lawyer looked at Richard's salary and his assets; he looked at his bills, which amounted to several thousands of dollars. The lawyer advised Richard to file for bankruptcy. Of course, it would mean he couldn't buy anything on credit for the next 10 years. Any purchases Richard made in the immediate future could be cash only. But maybe that was all for the better. Maybe he would do better paying as he went.

On Feb. 14, 1978, Richard filed a petition for bankruptcy with the U.S. District Court for the Western District of Michigan. Suddenly, he was out of debt. The ax was no longer looming over his head, ready to fall. Now Richard was free to get on with his life.

Richard realized better than anybody that, during the seven years since he walked out of Coldwater, he had made some mistakes. Life on the outside required a lot of knowledge and skill. Some of it Richard had learned the hard way. But that was OK. He had survived his misfortunes and had learned from them. He had a job and a nice place to live. He had friends. And, most importantly, he had his independence. Somehow he had landed on his feet. Again, Richard had everything he wanted.

As far as Richard knew at that point, his sole mission in life would be to hold onto what he had. His calling was to stay out of trouble and live a normal, independent life. With a way to earn a living, a decent place to sleep and a reasonable measure of freedom, Richard could be happy for the rest of his life. Maybe someday, way down the road, of course, he could reestablish his credit and buy a house with a lawn to mow and a garage where he could fix things. But that was a long-range goal toward which he would proceed cautiously. Richard had no inkling in the early summer of 1978 that the mission he had fashioned for himself soon would be replaced by a much more ambitious one.

As Richard settled into his life in Coldwater, as he became confident in his ability to find and keep work and shelter for himself, his perspective began to broaden. He knew he was lucky. The independence he was enjoying was being denied to thousands of people crippled by the system or deemed incapable for no good reason. Richard believed that as a victim of injustice who had been given the strength to rise above it, he had an obligation to do what he could to rescue other victims.

Richard Prangley, former resident of the Coldwater State Home and Training School, was about to become a media star, a player in state politics and a public crusader.

A Public Life

Governor Milliken said to me, "I like what you're doing, Richard." I told him I liked what he was doing, too.

— Richard Prangley

Richard's first big splash in the general-interest media came in August 1978, when Marti Rompf of the *Coldwater Daily Reporter* wrote a four-part series for the newspaper. It was billed as a general exploration of the mentally handicapped and their place in society. Although others were mentioned in Rompf's stories, Richard clearly stole the show. In fact, the headline on the second part of the series was "Richard Grows Up," and the headline on part 3 was "Richard Enters OUR Society."

Rompf's articles summarized the story of Richard's life — from his premature birth, to his success on the job at Essex Plastic and Metal — and held him up as an example of somebody who had prospered, despite the tragedy of extended institutionalization.

Richard made good copy. He was the common man who had been abused by the system and yet had managed to triumph over it. He was a victim of injustice who was determined to see justice prevail, not only for himself, but for others like him.

Rompf's stories painted a portrait of a man who had every right to be bitter, but instead was upbeat and likable. He had a humble, grateful demeanor and an innocent, almost childlike outlook on life. Much to any reporter's delight, Richard had a knack for serving up great quotes. It was no wonder that he would become the lead character in the series. Richard was a series in himself.

Rompf's stories piqued the interest of other newspaper and broadcast reporters, who came from nearby towns — and even from the major dailies in Detroit — to follow Richard while he made his rounds at Essex. They hung on his every word. They snapped pictures and rolled film. They nodded their heads in affirmation at the things he said.

Richard never turned a single reporter down. Why should he? All his life, people either didn't want to hear what Richard had to say, or listened with a polite tolerance — but only for so long. The reporters, on the other hand, were eager to hear what he had to say. They genuinely wanted to know about the abuses and injustices he had suffered in the institution across town. Even more surprisingly, they wanted to hear about his philosophy regarding deinstitutionalization and the rights of the developmentally disabled. And then they actually printed what he said.

Richard couldn't read the stories himself, but his friends read them to him. Richard was enthralled to hear his own words pouring out of their mouths. It was funny. Whenever Richard tried to tell his stories to the people he knew, their eyes glazed over and they tried to change the subject almost immediately. Richard's parents and siblings constantly told him to forget the past and get on with his life. The reporters, on the other hand, let Richard dig into the past as much as he wanted. They couldn't get enough of it. And Richard had more than enough to go around.

The publicity rekindled interest in Richard's movie — *Readin' and Writin' Ain't Everything*. Small groups around Coldwater began renting and showing the film. Suddenly, Richard was achieving celebrity status in Coldwater and, particularly, at the Essex factory. Most of his coworkers were amused and even impressed by Richard's celebrity status, but not all of them. His comments about the institution — in the newspapers and in the film — were not universally applauded.

Many of Richard's coworkers had relatives and friends who worked at the state home. Some of them had worked there themselves. They didn't like what Richard was saying about the things that happened there. Even if Richard was telling the truth about what took place long ago, that sort of thing didn't go on anymore, they said. What was in the past, was in the past. There was no point dragging it up again. It gave the whole town a black eye.

One man in particular confronted Richard in the employee lounge at Essex and told him that he should stop putting his nose where it didn't belong ... or else. Richard thought for a moment that the man was going to attack him physically. In fact, he was so troubled by the man's threats that he reported them to the personnel officer at Essex, who told the man to back off.

"Leave the past alone," the man told Richard. But Richard had no intention of doing any such thing.

Whether Richard became a casualty of his extracurricular activities or the downturn in Michigan's economy, he was laid off from his job at Essex. He went to work bussing tables at one Coldwater restaurant, then another one. As long as he was earning enough money to pay his rent and keep himself fed, Richard didn't care much that he was earning less than he had at Essex. His zeal for material possessions had waned since his bankruptcy. He began to realize the satisfaction he got from material possessions went only so far.

More and more, Richard began to think of other things — things that went beyond his determination to live a free and independent life surrounded by new furniture and television sets. By that point, Richard had convinced himself, once and for all, that he could make it on the outside. So far, despite the occasional setbacks, he had passed all the tests. He had proven that all those experts had underestimated him.

Richard began to realize, however, that the underestimation of the disabled was a tragedy that went beyond one man's struggle. He began to see that the Richard Prangley story was part of a much bigger picture. It was wrong to exclude people from the mainstream of society just because they learned differently from most people. Sure, he could make that point over and over again simply by thriving outside the institution — simply by living a productive life. But maybe that wasn't all he could do.

All those questions from the parade of reporters helped Richard develop the new perspective that had been creeping into his consciousness. He began to see his life in a larger context. The things he heard in church only bolstered the idea that human beings were human beings and that no group should be excluded from the mainstream of life. Richard was developing a missionary streak.

Then came the revelation.

In the summer of 1979, on Independence Day, to be exact, Richard was struck with an ambitious idea: the Michigan Mental Health Museum. In the vision that flashed before Richard like a bolt of lighting, he pictured a permanent exhibit documenting the horrors of the earliest approaches to the treatment of mental disabilities. The exhibit would show the progress made over the years, from the days of locking people up in asylums, to modern-day community placement. As Richard saw it, a museum devoted to documenting the mistakes of the past would be insurance against those mistakes being repeated.

Richard knew precisely when the idea took hold. Faced with a three-day holiday weekend and nothing much to do, Richard was killing time by wandering the grounds of the Coldwater institution.

Ironically, Richard found himself strolling among the institution's buildings frequently in those days. The grounds were within walking distance of his apartment. An ardent walker, Richard often set out on his long, rambling treks without a clear idea of a destination. More often than not, he ended up at the place that once so completely repelled him. Richard couldn't explain it, except to point out that now and then on those visits he ran into people he knew — not friends, exactly, but people with whom he shared memories. Beyond that, Richard's inclination to drift back to the institution was no more complicated, perhaps, than the lure of familiar spaces.

On July 4, Richard paused before the former administration building, that imposing brick structure with the Gothic facade. Richard didn't know at that point that the building had been scheduled for demolition. To him, it looked like the ideal place for the museum he had in mind. To Richard, his vision that day seemed nothing short of divine inspiration.

The way Richard had it figured, it must have been one of those guardian angels who nudged him toward the administration building that day, perhaps the same guardian angel who planted the notion in his head. A mental health museum. Suddenly Richard had a mission. He could hardly wait to tell the world about it.

By that time, the trend toward deinstitutionalization already was beginning. The Coldwater State Home and Training School had become the Coldwater Regional Center for Developmental Disabilities, and the number of residents had shrunk from more than 3,000 to about 700. The very year that Richard had his brainstorm, the Michigan legislature authorized $22 million to make the living quarters more homelike.

The cottages were reconfigured into small dormlike units, consisting of four bedrooms surrounding a common living area. Each bedroom was shared by two residents. And the living units were no longer numbered; they were named after trees. Cottage 11, for example, had become Elm, and Cottage 14 had become Pine. As for the old administration building, it had outlived its usefulness; it awaited the wrecking ball unless Richard could save it.

Richard began accumulating historical information about Coldwater. At the Branch County Library, Richard found another one of his guardian angels, a librarian willing to sit down with him three times a week and rummage through old local history books and records, piling up information about the institution. Richard also started to make tape recordings of his personal recollections of life in Cottage 41. Then he recruited another helper, a man from his church who helped Richard compose and mail letters to everyone who might contribute in any way to the rescue of the administration building and the creation of his museum.

Once the letters were flying toward their targets, Richard launched a lobbying blitz, his biggest campaign since his days in Grand Rapids when he managed to spring himself from the Hanson Home. This campaign would last 15 years. It would involve three governors, four Mental Health directors, and a supporting cast of characters too numerous to count.

That fall, Richard Schlaff, an aide to then Gov. William Milliken called Richard, "the most persistent person in the world."

Schlaff was quoted in the *Lansing State Journal:* "If he wants to sell you a 'Say Yes to Mental Health' button, you might as well say yes within three minutes, because eventually he'll sell you one."

The opening salvo of the campaign, Richard's letter, dated July 4, 1979 and addressed to "To Whom It May Concern," was simple and straightforward: "I, Richard Prangley, who was a resident [of the Coldwater State Home and Training

School] for 15 years, am interested in the development of the institution. I am also concerned about the historical significance to our community. Since the old administration building is not being used for housing or classes, could it be possible to have it remodeled to make it into a museum depicting the growth and changes of the institution itself? It could also reflect the history of the community."

Richard's letter went on to describe the kind of exhibits the museum would have, including one featuring residents "who were released and became productive citizens."

It wasn't an especially moving letter. Nor was it particularly eloquent. It was the kind of letter that would normally solicit polite, insincere replies from politicians and bureaucrats who were adept at saying no in 100 different ways, all of them polite. But within weeks, Richard was getting responses that were much more than brush-offs:

Aug. 22, 1979

Dear Mr. Prangley:
     Thank you for your letter to President and Mrs. Carter.
     Your idea for establishing a museum at Coldwater has much merit. If you haven't already done so, we suggest you share your proposal with David Rosen … of the Michigan Department of Mental Health.
     Best wishes in carrying out your ideas.
     Allen R. Menefee
     President's Committee on Mental Retardation.

Sept. 21, 1979

Dear Mr. Prangley:
     Thanks for writing about your plan to establish a public mental health museum at Coldwater Regional Center for Developmental Disabilities.
     Your idea of using a historic building to display memorabilia about Michigan's mental health care is an interesting one, worth careful thought. But, of course, it's a long way from idea to reality, especially when large amounts of money are involved.
     Mary Rave, who is now working with the Department of Mental Health on a long-range Community Relations program, is especially interested in your idea. She would be delighted to talk with you about it if you are going to be in Lansing soon.
     We hope your interest in the project will continue whatever the final decisions are, and we hope that you will be part of the planning group that studies the options and makes decisions.
     David Rosen

Richard's blizzard of letters touched off another blizzard of letters. Impressed with Richard's proposal, State Rep. Nick Smith, whose district included Coldwater, wrote to Gerald Miller, director of the state Department of Management and Budget under Gov. William Milliken, on Richard's behalf. Smith's letter to Miller, dated Aug. 10, 1979, said, in part:

> It has been suggested ... that the old Administration Building at the Coldwater Regional Center be converted into a museum. I request that you conduct a survey to establish construction estimates to renovate this building.
>
> I requested through the governor's office, and I repeat that request to you, that a "hold" be placed on the demolition of this building until such time when I receive your cost estimates and the feasibility of restoration.

In a lengthy reply to Smith's letter dated Sept. 24, Miller wrote in part:

> The message in your recent letter concerning the old Coldwater administration building, coming as it does from the writings of Richard Prangley and the related story from the Coldwater newspaper, is a poignant one. Certainly, the gulf of understanding between the experience of Mr. Prangley's childhood and youth and those of the rest of society is enormous. Efforts to bridge such a gulf are deserving of encouragement.
>
> However, a restoration of the old administration building as a museum may or may not be the most appropriate and effective means of spreading the message that the young Mr. Prangley so ably expresses.

Clearly, Miller was on the "may not" side. His letter went on to describe, in great detail, the obstacles in Richard's path:

> There are no state funds available for a historical museum at Coldwater. In view of the known history of the building, the physical problems that would be encountered are formidable, if not insurmountable. As early as 1943, six years before Richard Prangley was born, the building was surveyed by a registered architect, who reported that the building was decidedly submarginal and a fire hazard. It was again surveyed in 1969 — about 10 years after the east wing was destroyed by fire — at which time the surveyor, an architectural firm from Battle Creek, reported: "Whatever historical significance there was to this building is now destroyed. It would be a blessing to tear this building down and remove it from the premises."

Miller went on to explain that in 1976 the building was declared "vacant, unusable and was recommended for disposal." Miller stopped just short of declaring the project dead. He wrote: "The Bureau of Facilities will, however, proceed to survey the present condition of the facility and evaluate the physical (but not economic) feasibility of restoring it to a usable condition."

Because of Richard's letters and the stir they had caused in Lansing, demolition of the old administration building was officially postponed. The episode taught Richard that the buttons that needed to be pushed were not in Coldwater, but in the state capital. He decided that his best chance at getting his museum project off the ground was to go there to push the buttons himself.

In November 1979, on the brink of his 30th birthday, Richard moved into the YMCA on Lenawee Street, just a short walk from the Capitol. He knew about YMCAs from his first solo flight in Grand Rapids. Perhaps, he thought, the "Y" in Lansing would be as lucky for him as the one in Grand Rapids had been.

But before Richard even arrived in Lansing, the wheels already were in motion. For reasons not entirely explainable, a grandiose idea conceived by a janitor and former resident of an institution was causing a big ripple in the infamously inert bureaucracy. Why? Well, for one thing, Richard was the genuine article. He was no slick lobbyist trying to sell a package of smoke and mirrors. He was one man trying to do something good.

The people in charge were taking Richard seriously. More importantly, as Richard saw it, they were taking his idea seriously. Not that Richard was surprised by that. So profound was his belief in the value of a mental health museum that it seemed only natural to him that everybody else would adopt his vision. The most surprising thing to him, in fact, was that somebody hadn't already come up with the idea.

The interest generated by Richard's proposal went far beyond the exchange of letters and even beyond the postponement of the administration building's demolition. State Mental Health Director Frank Ochberg appointed a 12-member committee to study Richard's proposal. *A committee — to study and discuss Richard's brainstorm.* The committee included a special assistant to the governor and a director of a psychiatric hospital, mental health professionals and historians. And among the 12 was Richard himself. He barely had unpacked his bags at the YMCA when a letter arrived there from the Mental Health director:

> Dear Mr. Prangley:
> I am delighted that you are interested in being a member of the Committee to Determine the Feasibility of a Mental Health Museum. Thank you in advance for your help.
>   I am asking the committee to perform four specific tasks:
>   1. Consider what sites in Michigan would be appropriate for a mental health museum and make a recommendation;
>   2. Survey Department of Mental Health materials for potential displays in such a museum and make recommendations for what themes and kinds of displays would be interesting;

3. Explore options for funding; and

4. Determine what steps should be followed to establish such a museum, if you recommend that we pursue the idea.

Apparently, Ochberg's committee wasn't to concern itself with a question that arguably should have been at the top of the list: Would anybody actually visit a mental health museum? That question eventually would come under serious consideration, but not until years later.

Richard, for one, had no doubts. He was thrilled. Not only were some very important people taking his idea seriously, and not only were they actually going to have regular meetings to talk about it, but he, Richard Prangley, was going to be invited to the meetings. *He was going to be one of them.* He was going to help make the decisions.

That was the good news. The bad news was that the tide seemed to be turning against the administration building as a potential site for the museum. Richard couldn't read the letters going back and forth between the department heads and legislators, but he heard the talk. People were saying the administration building was too old and decrepit and that it would cost too much to renovate it.

Some very important people were going out of their way to break the news gently to Richard. While still living at the YMCA, Richard received a letter from Governor Milliken dated Dec. 27, 1979:

Dear Richard:

Thank you for your recent letter concerning the Administration Building at the Coldwater Regional Center.

I have reviewed much of the background on the building, including Dr. Gerald Miller's recommendation that it be demolished. I must reluctantly agree with his decision.

I feel that looking into the possibility of establishing a mental health museum is an excellent idea; however, it appears that the building at Coldwater is in such a state of disrepair that it would be very costly to bring it up to standard.

I understand that the building will not be demolished until after members of the museum committee have had a chance to personally view its condition.

You are doing an outstanding job on your project and are to be commended for all your time and efforts. I enjoyed meeting you at the Christmas reception at my office, and I do appreciate your writing to me. You have my best wishes for the new year.

Kind personal regards,

William G. Milliken

Richard was proud to get a letter from the governor, especially one that addressed him as "Richard," but he would have liked it more if the governor had been in his corner in the fight to save the administration building at Coldwater. With the governor on the other side, Richard could feel the odds tipping against his effort to salvage the old structure. But he wasn't quite ready to surrender. Maybe what he needed was a little more support. Maybe public opinion could reverse the trend. Maybe it was time to beat the publicity drum once again.

A Good Fight

I'm not the only one who got shafted by the system. Coldwater was full of people like me. I'm just trying to make sure that it never happens to any-body else again.

— Richard Prangley

In January of 1980, just a few days before his committee was to meet for the first time, Richard walked unannounced into the newsroom of the *Lansing State Journal* and told the receptionist that he had a good story to tell. The recep-tionist had heard that song more times than she could count and knew that the odds were against it. But that wasn't her problem. She relayed the information to the closest editor, who glanced over at the uncomfortable-looking man stand-ing in the doorway.

He was wearing blue jeans and a flannel shirt. He was a stocky man, about 5 feet, 9 inches tall. He appeared to be hunched over. He clutched a wad of papers. His eyes darted around the room like those of an animal out of its ele-ment. Another kook walking in off the street. Another victim of some imagined injustice. Another crackpot with an ax to grind. It was always the same; these peo-ple went to the cops, and when the cops quit listening, they came to the news-room. Maybe the cops sent them here as a joke. That would be just like the cops.

The editor took a deep breath, rolled her eyes and asked the man to sum-marize his beef. Briefly, please. The man started sputtering about a mental health museum he was trying to start and something about being wrongly institution-alized when he was just a kid. Sure, and most of the people serving time are inno-cent, just ask any reporter green enough to accept a collect call from a prison.

But Richard was used to people trying to brush him aside. It happened all the time; he'd speak a few sentences and the person he was speaking to would decide he wasn't "normal." Then the person would start edging away, nervously looking for an escape route. Richard developed a technique for pinning people down long enough for him to demonstrate that there was more to him than his odd mannerisms and awkward speech. It was a combination of sincerity and undeveloped but unmistakable self-confidence that lurked beneath the surface. He wasn't necessarily sure of himself, but he was absolutely convinced his mission was essential.

Richard knew the first impression he made always was a bad one. If he was ever going to get anywhere in life, he would have to get people to take a second look.

Richard persisted. The more he talked, the more the editor saw the possibility that maybe there really was a story there. She looked around for a reporter. That was one of the advantages of being an editor; you could pass people like that off to reporters, who were at the bottom of the newsroom pecking order. The reporters who had been enjoying the spectacle of the editor trying to extricate herself from the situation suddenly became very busy. Some had their telephone receivers at their ears; some were walking away quickly. One of the reporters wasn't quite quick enough. He was assigned to sit down with Richard and see if there was anything to what he was saying.

Richard had come armed with records and letters — not the daunting stack that some drop-ins bring to newsrooms; just enough to lend credence to his story. The reporter took the him into a conference room, offered him a chair and asked him if he wanted coffee. Yes, Richard said. Double cream; double sugar.

Richard started talking. His primary interest was his museum proposal and the rescue of the administration building, but he had spoken to enough reporters by then to know which parts of the Richard Prangley story most appealed to them. They always liked the horror stories from Coldwater — the abusive attendants, the violent residents — and they especially liked the angle that Richard never should have been in Coldwater in the first place. To Richard, the real story was the museum dream: the committee, the letters from the governor and imminent destruction of an historical landmark. But he knew that if he started with that bureaucratic stuff, he might lose the reporter. And besides, the museum angle might sound all the more impressive in the context of the story that preceded it.

Sure enough, the reporter locked onto Richard's assertion that he had been warehoused from the time he was 6 until he was 21 for no good reason. And it wasn't only Richard who was saying it. People with titles were saying it, too. Richard had letters saying it. Now that was one hell of a story, if it could be proven.

Confirmation, it so happened, was near at hand. Dr. Alex J. Cade, an East Lansing psychologist, evaluated Richard shortly after he arrived in Lansing, at the request of state officials investigating Richard's claims that he had been misdiagnosed at Coldwater. Contacted by the *State Journal* reporter working on the Prangley story, Cade said flatly: "In my opinion, Richard never belonged in an institution."

On Jan. 13, 1980, the *State Journal* ran a lengthy front-page story under the headline "Man Tries to Recover Lost Time." Cade was quoted extensively:

Richard, age 3.

Richard, age 6, at home in Jenison.

Richard, age 9, poses for a picture for his case record at the Coldwater State Home and Training School.

The old administration building at the Coldwater State Home and Training School.

Richard, age 13.

The outdoor play area of Cottage 41.

Richard worked on the farm at the Coldwater State Home. He was 19 when this photo was taken and proud to be a "working boy."

Richard, age 24.

Richard thriving and on his own in Grand Rapids.

Former Mental Health Director Frank Ochberg presents Richard with the Regional V HEW Handicapped Citizen of the Year Award in 1980.

Rep. Nick Smith, Richard, Frank Ochberg, and Martha Bigelow, former director of the Michigan History Commission, signing papers approving the historical marker Richard worked hard to bring into existence at Coldwater.

State Rep. Nick Smith (right) introduces Richard to Gov. William Milliken.

Mickey Rooney presents Richard with the 1984 Sackter Award.

Above: Richard and Gov. James Blanchard on the steps of the State Capitol, commemorating Michigan's 125th year of providing mental health services. Below: Former Mental Health Director C. Patrick Babcock, Governor Blanchard, and Richard with one of several commendations Richard received that day.

Richard at work.

Richard with Charles Wagg (center) and C. Patrick Babcock, both former directors of the Department of Mental Health.

Richard with former Mental Health Director Thomas Watkins Jr.

Richard poses with the Mental Health Educational Exhibit.

Richard became a familiar face at Oldsmobile Park, home of the Lansing Lugnuts.

Gov. John Engler, Richard, and Michigan Department of Community Health Director James Haveman Jr.

Richard and James Haveman celebrate Richard Prangley Day, June 20, 1995.

Richard at Disney World in 1992.

Richard and Mickey.

Richard and Manfred Tatzmann in front of the computer kiosk version of the mental health traveling exhibit.

Richard is an extreme example of the severe consequences of labeling people. He doesn't have (sophisticated) language skills; he doesn't have (sophisticated) social skills. But beneath the surface, there is considerable intelligence. He obviously has the ability to reason and think abstractly. I would have to assume he always had it.

His intelligence seems to be far greater than the category they put him in. He has tremendous ability to adapt, reason and adjust. If intelligence isn't the ability to adapt, reason and adjust, what is it?

Of course, it didn't take a psychologist to notice that the real Richard Prangley bore no resemblance to the boy described in the early records that Richard, already sensing a place for himself in mental health history, had begun to accumulate, even though he couldn't read them. This was the same person doctors described as an "imbecile" and a "moron," a person they said could not learn.

Now he was a wage-earning, tax-paying citizen, living a productive life outside the institution. More than that, his idea for a grand project was being taken seriously by powerful people. He was a valued and respected member of a state committee. He was getting letters addressed to "Richard" from the director of Mental Health and the governor. More astounding still, he was doing what many educated people believed was an impossible task; he was getting the state bureaucracy to act.

The *State Journal* article also quoted Richard's fellow committee member, Mary Rave: "Richard is supposed to be retarded, but the kind of political smarts he has is just mind-blowing."

Richard's strategy paid off once more. The front page story in the capital city newspaper touched off another flurry of publicity. The Associated Press picked up the piece, and soon reporters were standing in line to gather up Richard's best quotes. Politicians and bureaucrats eager to demonstrate they were friends of the underdog and enemies of injustice found ways to become associated with Richard Prangley. Like a political candidate launching a campaign, Richard sat back and admired the fuss his visit to the *State Journal* had created. It was just what he needed.

The Mental Health Museum Feasibility Committee met for the first time on January 15, 1980. Richard was the first to speak up: "A mental health museum would show people the history of treating the retarded and slow learners — like what happened to me. I hope this museum would be able to explain this issue so what happened to me doesn't happen to anybody else."

After listening to arguments for and against the old administration building as a possible site, the committee agreed to tour it on January 24.

In the end, neither the *State Journal* article nor the tour to Coldwater stopped the wrecking ball. The committee, after visiting the Coldwater administration building, ultimately sided with the bean counters. Turning the 110-

year-old building into a museum would cost too much, especially for a state in a recession. The committee wrote:

> The group was impressed by the historic and architectural features of the structure. With genuine regret, the committee had to dismiss the Old Administration Building as a museum site for several reasons. They include the extensive deterioration of the structure and high cost of restoration; its size and high ceilings and concomitant utility costs and mainly, the factor that necessary funds could not be raised in time to save the building from scheduled and contracted demolition.
>
> The committee unanimously regrets the disappearance of this impressive example of latter 19th-century architecture.

In March 1980, committee members voted to rescind the stay of execution. The old ad building was razed the following month.

As always, Richard was good for a quote.

"My heart is in that building," he told the *State Journal.* "If I had the money, you bet I would save that building. I'd put $5 million in if I had it."

It had been a good fight, and though Richard had lost the battle, the war was far from over. Richard did, however, come out of the process with something. The following year, he presided over the dedication of a historical marker on the Coldwater grounds. It so happened that the United Nations General Assembly declared 1981 the International Year of the Disabled Person.

As part of Michigan's recognition of the UN's declaration, the institution at Coldwater was officially designated an historical site and a marker was erected. The $1,200 cast-aluminum monument, bearing an inscription describing some of the institution's history, was paid for through private contributions. Richard kicked in the first $35, then raised the rest of the money.

A lengthy editorial in the *Coldwater Daily Reporter* relayed some of Richard's adventures in raising the money:

> Richard arrived at the Reporter office with a grand total of $379.58. This money he raised himself by attaching a copy of a Mental Health Department news release to a collection can. He then solicited funds, a dime here and a quarter there, from the Mental Health offices and his Lansing church.
>
> Beaming with pride, Richard informed us he needed only $820.42 more for the plaque to become a reality. After safely depositing those funds in the Historical Marker Fund at a local bank, Richard had lunch with Coldwater businessman Lee Feller, a long-time Prangley supporter.
>
> Two or three hours later, Richard returned to our office again, this time with another $65, which bumped the overall total to $444.58.

It still looked hopeless to us, but we had to admire the guy's spunk. He was as positive as could be and returned to Lansing, assured the October 1981 plaque installation date could still be met.

The following day Richard called us again. He had reached his goal! It seems that after [a] bus ride to Battle Creek, he found his way to the office of the Battle Creek Enquirer and News. There he learned about the Miller Foundation, which contributes funds to projects such as the one he was pursuing.

The day after his Coldwater visit, officials from the Miller Foundation contacted Prangley and told him they would make up the difference from what he had collected already, or just under $800.

Having conceived of the project and having raised the money to pay for the marker, it was only fitting that Richard would also help determine what the marker would say. Richard wanted more than platitudes. At his insistence, the inscription outlines the history of the facility from 1871 to 1978.

The dedication of the marker took place 18 months later. Richard was invited to say a few words. Once again, he saw an opportunity to impress his parents. As the date for the dedication approached, Richard, with the help of a friend, wrote to John and Dorothy Prangley:

Dear Mom and Dad:
I still think a lot about you. Perhaps you wonder why I haven't called or come to visit you as much as I should. I have been busy working on a project relating to the International Year of Disabled Persons.

I happen to be on the IYDP Committee working to make things better for the handicappers. I'm working on a project for Coldwater Regional Center for Developmental Disabilities and we are placing a historical marker there at the facility. I will be dedicating this marker.

One of the things taking place there is that I will be giving a presentation speech and I would like to invite both of you, my mom and dad, to participate at this dedication ceremony at the Coldwater Regional Center.

If you have any further questions and if you are interested in coming, call me and let me know next week so I can inform the Department of Mental Health as to who is coming.

The Prangleys were not among the guests. For reasons never explained, they missed Richard's oratorical debut.

Richard didn't let his disappointment spoil his moment in the spotlight. As always, he performed with a flourish. His speech ended this way: "I say unto you, let this now be a new beginning on the mental health frontier."

The marker wasn't the only thing Richard gained from the campaign to save the ad building. He also came out of it with a reputation. Richard graduated from mental-health-system-survivor-with-a-poignant-story-to-tell, to phenomenon. As Mary Rave had pointed out, the man had political smarts. He might have been a slow learner in some areas, but he was clearly an overachiever when it came to cultivating political favor. He had the rare gift of being charming while being persistent. He could be a pit bull, but people always wanted to reach down and pet him.

In Lansing, where political instincts are revered, Richard became the toast of the town, the darling of the power elite. He was no longer just a friend to movers and shakers. He was a mover and shaker. He landed a state job; first in maintenance with the Department of Management and Budget, and later in the mailroom of the Department of Mental Health. But it was his avocation, not his job, that kept him going.

In a letter dated March 17, 1980, director Ochberg added to his boss's knowledge of Richard:

> Dear Governor Milliken:
>
> Richard Prangley is a phenomenon. He was tragically hospitalized at the Coldwater facility for 15 years, diagnosed as an "imbecile," when his real problem was a moderate learning disorder, which could have responded to aggressive special education.

Ochberg went on to say that Richard had distinguished himself as a "model patient," which was true only if you looked exclusively at Richard's final year at Coldwater.

The director's letter went on to laud Richard's museum idea as "dramatic and creative."

Finally, Richard's efforts to launch the museum earned him his first award: Handicapped Citizen of the Year — 1980, in a six-state area. The award was sponsored by the U.S. Department of Health and Human Services. In making the nomination, Ochberg wrote:

> Although Mr. Prangley can neither read nor write, he has accomplished more in the nine years since he left Coldwater than many less handicapped people do in a lifetime.
>
> He was persistent in his appeals for the museum. Not willing to take no action for an answer, he plagued and cajoled the department director, legislators, the governor's staff and the governor himself. He wrote to Rosalynn Carter for support and contacted Walter Mondale through a mutual acquaintance.

Ever quotable, Richard told the press that the chief value of the award was that it called attention to his main message: that mentally disabled people could be valuable, contributing citizens. And, as always, he meant it.

Aside from his successes in his public life, Richard was making great strides in his personal life as well. When he first arrived in Lansing, he was collecting unemployment compensation. It was a juicy irony. This was the man who was getting letters from the governor and other heads of state, the man whose idea merited a full-blown committee, the man who was sitting at the same table with pillars of the establishment studying *his* proposal. And he was drawing unemployment compensation. Maybe the irony was little *too* juicy.

Richard took advantage of his spare time to explore the offices in the Capitol. He became a frequent visitor at State Rep. Nick Smith's office. After Richard's splash in the *Coldwater Daily Reporter,* Smith had taken an interest in Richard and his museum proposal. Believing that the state owed Richard something, Smith pulled a few strings and got Richard a job working for the State of Michigan, doing janitorial work in the Lewis Cass Building in downtown Lansing. No Civil Service test was required.

A couple of months later, Smith told Richard that he wanted to introduce him to somebody. Richard followed Smith down a corridor and through some impressive doors, and soon he was shaking hands with Governor Milliken. Richard and the governor had a nice chat about Richard's museum project and his hopes for the future. The very next day, Richard kept an appointment in the personnel office of the Department of Mental Health. Director Ochberg instructed the employees there to help Richard with the necessary paperwork.

Suddenly, Richard was off mop duty and working in the mailroom of the Office Services Unit of the Department of Mental Health. The rumor was that Milliken had personally ordered Ochberg to find Richard a job in his department and that it was a lifetime appointment. Richard's job description, outlined in a memo dated July 9, 1980, was as follows:

1. Maintain Xerox copier (change paper, etc.) and learn operation.
2. Assist in storing stock and supplies.
3. Assist in arranging shelves where stock and supplies are stored.
4. Assist in packaging forms.
5. Assist in preparation of mail (hand stamp special envelopes, stapling of materials, etc.)
6. Accompany mail courier on rounds to Capitol and Commerce Center and make special trips on his own, as appropriate, to deliver and pick up special mail between Cass Building and Commerce Center.

And so on. In all, 13 specific duties were mentioned. It was a new job description for a new position. In fact, Richard's job didn't fit any of the Michigan Civil Service System's existing classifications. The architects of his payback from the State of Michigan solved that problem by creating a new classification. Richard became a classification of one.

It was a minor job in a large department, and yet everybody, including the director, seemed to be bending over backward to make sure Richard Prangley felt comfortable. The other employees in the department took note of it. It only added to Richard's mystique as a man with friends in high places. In case there was any doubt of that, Governor Milliken dropped by the department once or twice in the first few weeks to ask Richard how he was getting on.

This special attention didn't always serve Richard well, where his fellow employees were concerned. Although some were ready to take Richard under their wings, others were resentful of the special attention he got. It was always Richard who got the pats on the back from the bosses.

It was always Richard who got special permission to take time off to go give a speech or attend a conference. Clearly, Richard was the teacher's pet. Despite the resentments and the distractions, Richard did what he always had done. He rolled up his sleeves and went to work, always performing his duties meticulously. The mailroom job would become Richard's long-term, steady day job. The job paid only slightly more than minimum wage, but it was a way for Richard to keep his bills paid while he went about his real work of changing the world.

Richard stayed at the YMCA for about eight months and might have stayed there longer if it hadn't been for the break-in. While Richard was gone one day, somebody picked the lock on his door and stole his tape recorder — the one he had been using to record his recollections of life at Coldwater. In the months since he had conceived of the mental health museum, Richard had recorded hours and hours of his memories of life inside the institution, as well as impressions and philosophies regarding the place of the disabled in society.

No longer secure at the "Y," Richard moved into a single room in a house just a few blocks down the street from the "Y." From there, Richard moved into a room on the third floor of the Plaza Hotel, which was right across the street from the Capitol. The Plaza, which offered rooms by the month, was a haven for lobbyists who wanted to remain close to the action. Richard stayed there for two years. When he wasn't on his job in the nearby Lewis Cass building or rubbing elbows with lawmakers at the Capitol, he was exploring downtown Lansing on foot, learning the city bus system and planting the seeds of what would become long-lasting attachments.

One of Richard's early discoveries in Lansing was one of the city's oldest restaurants, Clara's — a converted train depot not far from downtown on the city's main street, Michigan Avenue. Richard liked the atmosphere and down-to-earth cooking at Clara's, and the management and staff there took to the friendly, gentle, polite man who almost always came in alone and always seemed to be in a good mood. On the first day Richard stepped into Clara's, he got the feeling that the hospitality there was genuine. Immediately, it became his favorite restaurant.

Peter Jubeck, it so happened, had taken over the restaurant about the same time Richard arrived in Lansing. As Richard became a regular at Clara's, Jubeck took an interest in him and eventually became aware of Richard's history. Like most people who bothered to look beneath the surface of the man with the awkward speech and manners, Jubeck came to like Richard.

Taking their cue from the boss, the waiters gave Richard VIP treatment every time he came in. Over the years, the relationship blossomed beyond the conventional proprietor-customer arrangement.

Richard always sat at the same table, number 30, in an out-of-the-way niche of the restaurant, where he could hold court without interrupting the flow of things. Primarily a meat-and-potatoes man, Richard almost always ordered steak or pork chops. But sometimes he surprised his waiter by ordering a Polynesian Tuna Melt.

Eventually, the all-you-can-eat buffets would test Richard's loyalties, but he always returned to Clara's at least once a week. It was like going home.

But Richard's most important attachment was his relationship with Manfred Tatzmann, who, over the years, became Richard's mentor, confidante, teacher, agent and best friend. Tatzmann, who was a few years older than Richard, would become the father–big brother that Richard never really had. Over the next five years, Richard would become the younger brother Tatzmann never had. Even after Tatzmann moved to Marquette as the Mental Health Department's area manager for the Upper Peninsula, he remained Richard's best friend.

Tatzmann's career in the department began in the summer of 1980. A member of Governor Milliken's staff at the time, Tatzmann was sent over to Mental Health for what was supposed to be a temporary stint. His mission was to help the new director, Frank Ochberg, with his transition and to guide the department through the precarious times immediately ahead.

It was a precarious summer and fall for the people in state government. A once-obscure drain commissioner from Shiawassee County named Robert Tisch rose to prominence with a plan to slash Michigan property taxes by 60 percent and require 60 percent voter approval to add fees or taxes or increase the ones already in existence. Tisch gathered enough signatures on petitions to force a vote. His plan would show up on the November ballot as Proposal D.

Like most government officials, Milliken believed Proposal D would spell disaster for the people of Michigan, and, particularly, for the disadvantaged. He became one of the generals in the anti-Tisch coalition, which adopted the name sos (Save Our State). Part of the campaign strategy was to have various experts point out what Tisch's massive budget cuts would do to the consumers of state services. Tatzmann's main role was to help circle the wagons in Mental Health. Ultimately, Proposal D was defeated at the polls.

Tatzmann was in his office one day when a department employee approached and asked him for an "opinion" on something. The man explained he was new in the department and that he had received a letter he didn't quite understand. He wondered if Tatzmann would take a look at it and perhaps offer some clarification. As Tatzmann began to read the letter, half out loud and half to himself, it became obvious to him that the man in fact *hadn't* read the letter because he couldn't read.

The man was, in a sense, conning Tatzmann. But Tatzmann wasn't put out by it; he was, in fact, impressed with the man's ingenuity. He began asking questions about Richard. He learned about Richard's 15 years at Coldwater and his determination to live a productive, independent life. Tatzmann heard about Richard's evolution from institutionalization to advocacy and his attempt to create a mental health museum. And, of course, Tatzmann quickly became aware of Richard's connections to people in high places, including Tatzmann's boss.

Ironically, on the day Richard walked up to him and asked him to clarify the letter, Tatzmann wasn't aware that a relationship existed between Milliken and the mail clerk. Meanwhile, Richard, who was always on the lookout for a new friend, quickly developed the habit of stopping at Tatzmann's desk and chatting. Tatzmann immediately took to Richard's honesty and enthusiasm. The more Tatzmann heard, the more he liked Richard. The more he got to like him, the more inclined he was to look out for Richard's interests.

Tatzmann quickly became known throughout the department as the Richard Prangley expert. Telephone calls for Richard, from talk-show hosts and reporters, from seminar organizers and arrangers of panel discussions, often went straight to Tatzmann.

Eventually, Richard began running all of his major decisions past Tatzmann before he made them. One of the early ones involved Richard's living arrangements. While staying at the Plaza, Richard learned of a housing opportunity that intrigued him. A man Richard knew told him about the bottom floor of a large, old two-story house that had become available. It was within walking distance of his job and the Capitol. For not much more than he was paying for a single room at the Plaza Hotel, Richard could have a half-dozen rooms and a basement.

It wasn't that Richard was losing interest in the museum project and the lobbying it required. He still considered himself a full-time advocate for the mentally disabled. He had every intention of continuing his work of hammering away at the bureaucrats for however long it took. But everybody, including Tatzmann, had been telling Richard he needed a little balance in his life.

His friends, or, rather, the people who came the closest to the definition of "friend," had been telling Richard his constant preaching about mental health sometimes wore a little thin. It was good to be dedicated to a cause, but nobody enjoyed being around somebody who beat the same drum over and over again. Most people preferred more variety.

Lobbying and socializing, Tatzmann told him, were two different things. If Richard were serious about his desire to socialize, he would have to learn how and when to move on to other topics.

In fact, the art of conversation was something Richard would continue to struggle with. It would take him many years and much practice to understand the difference between preaching and conversation; between lecturing and conversation; between spouting slogans and conversation; between sound bites and conversation. Throughout his early years outside Coldwater, Richard developed a spiel, a standard story to explain and define himself. It included some dramatic memories of his life inside the institution, some pithy observations about the inhumanity of institutions in general and some highly quotable statements on the future of mental health care.

It was a stock speech, tested and refined on the army of reporters who set out to tell the Richard Prangley story. Break out a notebook or put a microphone in Richard's face, and Richard was on solid ground. He knew exactly what to say; he was as reliable a quote machine as any political candidate. For public consumption, it worked well. His story was a tragedy, yes, but a sanitized one. By the process of trial and error, Richard discovered what worked and what didn't work. He learned that the reporters wanted some pain and suffering, but not too much. They especially liked the part about the human spirit's triumph over injustice and injury.

It was easy to see how Richard, unschooled in social conventions and unfamiliar with the process by which friendships are formed, deduced that since his material worked so well for TV and print, it would work equally well in one-on-one situations. What's more, it was a way Richard could control the conversation. As long as he defined the parameters, he didn't have to worry about where the conversation might lead. As long as he limited the discourse to the Richard Prangley everybody knew, he could avoid talking about the other Richard Prangley — the man with the secrets.

Cracking that shell would be a long-range project. Meanwhile, Richard began to see that maybe it wasn't such a good idea to be living in a hotel so close to the Capitol. Maybe it caused him to stay too keenly focused on his work. In his own house, he could relax. He could mow the lawn, rake leaves and shovel snow. He could plant flowers and, best of all, he could use the basement for a workshop. Maybe he could even take up a hobby or two, or get back to the woodworking he enjoyed so much in his last year at Coldwater. Then, at least, he could talk to people about planting grass and putting up wallpaper and fixing furniture.

Richard signed a lease and moved in. He remained in the house for eight years—the longest he lived anywhere, except for the institution. He loved it. Once the landlord, an elderly woman who lived upstairs, observed Richard's meticulousness firsthand, she had no objections to the improvements Richard proposed.

This was a whole new phase of freedom for Richard. For the first time, he was free to not only enjoy his little patch of independence, but he actually could alter it to suit his tastes without having to abide by, or even solicit, a second opinion. Richard planted shrubs and flowers; he built a wooden fence; he painted and remodeled the basement. He hung the pictures he liked exactly where he wanted them. And once he had renovated and redecorated the space immediately around him, he looked beyond it; his missionary zeal took a new direction.

Richard couldn't help but notice that not all his neighbors shared his meticulousness. He thought they should. In December 1986, Richard enlisted the help of a coworker in composing a letter to the Lansing City Council:

> During the 2 ½ years that I have lived in the neighborhood … I have been trying to maintain my home and keep my yard in good, clean condition. With 1987 being the Sesquicentennial year, I intend to do some revitalization and remodeling around my home…. I would like to see something done to require landlords to fix up their properties and maintain them.
>
> I realize that I cannot do much about the neighbors not raking their lawns, but what can I do to get the city to force these people to clean up their yards? I work diligently to maintain my property and yard and it is very frustrating to find the rest of the neighborhood in such poor condition.

Untidy neighbors and all, Richard came to like the house so much that after he was there for a few years, and after he had invested his money and time in improving the place, he and the owner made an informal arrangement for Richard to buy the house one day. However, the owner died unexpectedly and the deal never came to fruition.

It was in that house that Richard launched the many collections that would one day threaten to consume every inch of every flat surface in his various dwellings. As it turned out, the desire to own things that contributed to Richard's financial difficulties in Grand Rapids hadn't expired; it merely had lain dormant while he was hopping from Grand Rapids, to Detroit, to Ypsilanti, to California, to Coldwater, then, finally, to Lansing.

It didn't take any deep psychological insights to understand Richard's impulse to acquire things. He himself understood it was a reaction to his life at the institution, where he had virtually nothing to call his own. In Grand Rapids, it took the form of televisions and stereos and furniture. In Lansing, it took a form less likely to cause hardship.

First came the ducks.

Richard's dentist, it so happened, had an office near the Red Cedar River. Richard made it a point to stroll along the river before and after dental appointments. He liked the peacefulness of the lazy Red Cedar, and he particularly liked the ducks that always swarmed toward him, looking for handouts.

Richard started buying ducks in the flea markets and thrift shops around Lansing — ceramic ducks, wooden ducks, stuffed ducks, crystal ducks; ducks on pillows and in paintings and on glassware. He even bought a duck telephone. It didn't ring; it quacked.

Before he knew it, Richard had 200 of them competing for space on his tables and counters and bookshelves. They even fanned out in formations across his living room carpet.

The ducks were only the first of many collections. Richard went on to accumulate Star Trek memorabilia, Walt Disney paraphernalia and Coca-Cola trinkets. He filled an entire room with objects commemorating the Michigan sesquicentennial. Soon he had a vast collection of collections.

Richard's appetite for bric-a-brac seemed boundless. Although his possessions soon threatened to take over every inch of his flat, no one could ever accuse Richard of being disorderly. Everything had its place. Ducks filled his dining room table. Frisbees hung from his walls like oil paintings. If his apartment looked like a flea market, it was always an extremely neat flea market.

While others may have looked for a connection between Richard's urge to fill every square inch of his apartment with things and his inability to call anything his own during his 15 years inside the institution, Tatzmann always shrugged off the clutter as Richard's "style." Tatzmann saw it as a healthy assertion of Richard's independence. As Tatzmann saw it, if Richard wanted to hang Frisbees on the walls of his living room, he had earned the right to do so.

Looking back at those days of the late 1970s and early 1980s, those who were there for Richard's debut in state politics and his subsequent blossoming as a full-fledged citizen agree it was a remarkable episode. They attribute it to a combination of factors, beginning with Richard's belief in his vision, but quickly leading to Governor Milliken's style of leadership in general and his personal interest in Richard in particular.

Mental Health director Ochberg had been appointed by Milliken in the summer of 1979. Before that, Ochberg, a psychiatrist, was associate director for crisis management at the National Institute of Mental Health. After just two years as Mental Health director, Ochberg left government and became a practicing psychiatrist in Okemos, a suburb of Lansing, and an adjunct professor at Michigan State University.

Reflecting on Richard's swift ascent from obscurity to celebrity status, Ochberg, speaking 15 years after he left the Mental Health Department, said the fact that a busy governor's attention could be captured by one man with a poignant story and a sincere desire to improve the world was indicative of Milliken's philosophy of government. Said Ochberg:

> The governor was supportive of Richard in an extremely personal way. I think it was consistent with the kind of governor Milliken was. He came to government to do good things. The institutions of the state had hurt Richard Prangley and, because Milliken was part of government, he felt personally responsible for it. He felt the state owed Richard something.
>
> Milliken believed that government should be an instrument of compassion and he surrounded himself with people who shared that philosophy. That's why I came to Michigan. It fit with my values and principles. I thought we should bring into government — and into the mental health system — people who were hurt by the system, people who were on the wrong side of the keys.

C. Patrick Babcock, who served as both Labor director and Mental Health director under Milliken, said it was not at all unusual for his boss to become engaged in spontaneous discussions with people who showed up outside his office, unannounced, wishing to discuss their problems. Interviewed in 1996, Babcock said: "It used to drive his staff nuts, because you couldn't get [Milliken] to come to meetings on time. He had a strong commitment to people. He thought a lot about whether government was really reaching the people who had problems."

Babcock believed Milliken's natural inclination to become involved in the problems of real people, combined with Richard's persistence and skill at making his case, made the difference. Of course, it didn't hurt that the story itself was compelling.

Interviewed in 1996, Milliken recalled being struck by the basic unfairness of what had happened to Richard.

After seeing some of the letters that Richard had been grinding out, Milliken asked his staff to look into the case and see if there was anything to the man's claims that he had been inappropriately warehoused for 15 years. His staff looked into the matter and concluded that, indeed, Richard's claims were true. Said the former governor: "My strong impression was that Richard got caught in the bureaucratic machinery. His story seemed to me to be a tragic example of the failure of the system to serve as it was intended to serve. I felt quite deeply about it. We decided to try to find some way to pay him back a little."

Milliken remembered Richard as a regular in the halls of the Capitol. After the formal introduction by Representative Smith, Richard frequently dropped by the governor's office, unannounced. He didn't know enough about protocol to realize that one didn't just drop by the office of a governor and actually expect to see him. But Milliken wasn't overly impressed with protocol himself. If he happened to be in his office, and if he had a spare minute or two, the governor invited Richard in for a chat. Milliken came to admire Richard's determination and enterprise and often took the opportunity to encourage him in his personal and public goals.

Inside the System

*I don't care if I'm dealing with a Republican or a Democrat. I don't care.
As long as he goes along with what I'm trying to do.*

— *Richard Prangley*

While Richard's personal life was gathering steam, his museum idea was
mired in bureaucratic mud and growing indifference. The Museum Feasibility Committee met five times in the first three months of 1980. After considering and touring four possible sites for the museum, including the old
administration building at Coldwater, the committee concluded, by a process
of elimination, that the best place for the museum would be the Traverse City
Regional Psychiatric Center.

Located in the northwest section of Michigan's lower peninsula, Traverse
City, the committee noted, already was a tourist destination. It attracted boaters
in the summer; skiers in the winter. Also, the hospital, the committee noted,
already possessed the state's only known collection of equipment used for the
treatment of the emotionally ill.

In true bureaucratic form, the Feasibility Committee recommended that
the ball be passed to an "Implementation Committee" that would carry the
project through its next phase. That committee would, among other things, try
to figure out a way to pay for the museum.

The Feasibility Committee's final report recommended "that the name of
the museum should include the name of Richard Prangley because of his sustained efforts to make a mental health museum a reality and because he represents an example of the intellectual potential so often overlooked in the education of impaired learners. Also, it is hoped that he will be considered to serve as
a consultant to the projected museum."

But, in truth, the museum proposal seemed to be in serious jeopardy. The
project was running out of gas. By late 1981, with Michigan heading toward a
full-blown recession and government leaders scrambling to protect their budgets
and their scalps, even those among the dwindling ranks still willing to help

Richard fulfill his dream were modifying their goals. Sentiment was beginning to turn away from a full-fledged museum and toward something less ambitious.

Meanwhile, Richard was losing some key allies. In July 1981, exactly two years after Ochberg accepted the job as the state's Mental Health director, he resigned, under pressure. Some said the director was spending too much time on matters outside Michigan. A nationally recognized expert on hostage situations, Ochberg acted as a consultant to the federal government during the 1979 Iranian hostage crisis, when Americans were held at the U.S. Embassy in Tehran. Ochberg also worked with the FBI, the U.S. Secret Service and Scotland Yard. Critics, mostly in the state legislature, said Ochberg was too frequently out making headlines on high-profile cases when he should have been home in Michigan, minding the store.

Also, a state audit castigated Ochberg for "questionable and costly" travel expenses. Finally, some Ochberg critics, both in the legislature and in the Mental Health Department, thought Ochberg was going too fast in moving mental patients out of large institutions and into community settings.

Milliken chose Ochberg's chief deputy, C. Patrick Babcock, to take over as director. Babcock, who had been director of the state Department of Labor, had been the chief deputy only 30 days when he was asked to take the reins from Ochberg. Babcock would keep the job for six years.

Babcock knew a little about Richard even before he became part of the Mental Health establishment. He had followed newspaper stories about the former Coldwater resident, and Babcock couldn't help but be intrigued by a man who was accomplishing a rare maneuver: rocking the boat and making powerful friends at the same time. Babcock also had seen Richard hanging around the office of his boss, the governor, who frequently, Babcock noticed, made time for the mail clerk. Babcock had hardly settled into the director's office when Richard, eager to size up his new boss, came calling.

Some members of the Mental Health Department staff might have been going through a period of mourning for Ochberg, but Richard wasn't among them. Not that Richard hadn't liked and admired the former director. Ochberg had been instrumental in the start-up phase of the mental health museum project, and Richard was grateful for everything Ochberg had done to get the thing off the ground. But Ochberg was gone. Milliken was gone, too. In fact, all the people who had nurtured Richard's fledgling idea to create a mental health museum had moved on to other assignments and projects.

The original committee had broken up and disbursed. The rubble of the old administration building at Coldwater had been swept up and carted away. The initial momentum was gone. But Richard was still there, ready to recruit a new following. The mission had a long way to go, and Richard was well aware of the fact that the new Mental Health director would be a key factor in accomplishing it. To Richard, it didn't matter so much who that director was. Republican or Democrat. Conservative or Liberal. Old guard or new. The important thing was that he shared Richard's vision for the future.

Richard didn't mind starting from the beginning. He spoke to Babcock about the conditions inside Coldwater and, by extension, the other state institutions. He patiently explained that the museum was necessary to insure a more enlightened approach to mental disabilities and illnesses by showing exactly how and where the old approach of locking people away had failed.

Richard didn't have to do much convincing. He was preaching to the choir. His new boss was well aware of the fact that institutionalization had its limitations. Babcock already was a believer in community placement. That was part of why Milliken chose him to guide the department into a new era. Babcock remembered the figures long after he left state government. When he first met Milliken, 24,000 people lived inside state institutions for the mentally ill and disabled. By the time Milliken left office, that number was down to less than 4,000.

Clearly, both men saw Richard as an embodiment of their philosophy of mainstreaming. The more Babcock got to know Richard, the more certain he felt he and his boss were on the right course. Both Milliken and Babcock were struck by the fact that if Richard had been born in 1979, instead of 1949, he would never have seen the inside of the Coldwater State Home and Training Center, or any other institution. Obviously, the man had intelligence. To realize that, all anybody had to do was look at the adaptive mechanisms he had developed. Babcock would later say, "If you want to find a good indictment of the institutional system, just take a look at Richard Prangley."

Babcock couldn't help but notice, however, that not all of his lieutenants shared his belief in the wisdom of dismantling the institutional system. Some of the administrators, people who were still part of the old system, became edgy when Richard waltzed into the director's office and started criticizing the way things had been done in the past. It was a sensitive time in the department. The debate over institutionalization versus community placement was heating up. Some of the top administrators had spent their entire careers building and staffing the institutions. Many of the things Richard was saying made them uneasy. It called into question their life's work.

Babcock and the other advocates of the new approach understood the importance of proceeding slowly, of employing tact and diplomacy along the way. Richard knew only one tactic: full speed ahead.

Why waste time on tact and diplomacy? Why beat around the bush? Richard knew that eventually everybody would see the light. It was just a matter of time.

In 1982, Milliken didn't seek reelection. The Republicans ran tax-reformer Dick Headlee, a Detroit-area businessman, but he was defeated by Democrat James Blanchard. Blanchard kept Babcock as his Mental Health director. Babcock often said, at least half jokingly, that it was Richard who got him reappointed. Richard, he said, had Blanchard "scoped out" before the election. In any case, Babcock's reappointment was a stroke of luck for Richard, who would develop a personal relationship not only with the director, but also with his wife, Patricia, whom Richard called "Patty."

Richard became a frequent guest at the Babcock home. One memorable Halloween night, Richard went out trick-or-treating with the Babcock children. Never had Richard seen anything like it. He was awestruck by the whole spectacle: the hordes of kids in costumes, the trek through the neighborhood, the jack-o'-lanterns.

Every aspect of the celebration fascinated Richard. At one point in the evening, he became so caught up in the spirit than he began chasing some of the smaller children on the street while making scary noises. The Babcocks had to dampen Richard's enthusiasm a little, explaining to him that adults participated in Halloween a little differently than children did. It didn't stifle Richard's taste for Halloween. Every year thereafter, the days leading up to Halloween would find Richard's apartment elaborately decorated with jack-o'-lanterns, skeletons and black cats.

While Patrick nurtured Richard on the job, Patricia set out to help him gain ground in his personal life. Manfred Tatzmann was well acquainted with the Babcocks because of their mutual ties to the Milliken administration. He knew Patrick even before they both became part of the Mental Health Department. Aware of the fact that Patty had a background in education, Tatzmann brought Richard to the Babcocks' Lansing home one evening.

Tatzmann specifically wanted to introduce Richard to Patty. She held a degree in school counseling. Manfred, whose interest in Richard's welfare was deepening in those days, asked Patty if she knew somebody who might be willing to work with Richard as a reading tutor. Manfred knew that while Richard had developed ingenious coping mechanisms to compensate for his illiteracy, his inability to read and write continued to hold him back, particularly on the job. Tatzmann felt certain that Richard had the intellectual tools to learn how to read. All he needed, Tatzmann figured, was some intensive one-on-one tutoring.

Patty, it so happened, was looking for a project. She volunteered to take the job. It was a serious commitment of time and energy. Patty established a plan. Almost every Sunday night, she would drive into downtown Lansing, pick Richard up at the Plaza Hotel, bring him to the Babcock house, then sit with him at the dining room table for a couple of hours and labor with him over the basics of reading and writing. That went on for two years, over which time Richard gained very little ground, at least in reading and writing.

Eventually, Richard sensed that the experiment wasn't working. The frustrations he felt 10 years earlier, when his brother tried to teach him to read, came back to him. He became impatient with the lessons and would squirm like a schoolboy on a spring afternoon. Finally, Patty would release him and he was free to pursue Patrick in some other corner of the house, where he would talk shop with his boss. Richard couldn't resist the opportunity for some moonlight schmoozing.

By the time the tutoring was over, Patty sincerely believed she learned more from Richard than he learned from her. She said it was more, in fact, than she ever had learned from another human being. Patty was mostly fascinated by Richard's total disregard for limits. She saw him as a person who would, for example, invite the governor out to lunch, or ask Nancy Reagan to endorse an idea of his, never stopping to worry about the unlikelihood of powerful and important people accepting his invitations. Not being encumbered by self-censorship, Richard would scatter his invitations to the wind, like seeds, and a certain percentage of them would find fertile ground. Other people would be amazed at his success. They would wonder how Richard Prangley got such important people to do what he asked. The answer was because he always expected them to.

Richard and Patty never made much headway in cracking the mysteries of the written word, but Patty helped Richard in other ways. She noticed, for example, he did all of his grocery shopping in small quantities at convenience stores. Patty explained to Richard that he could save money and time by buying larger quantities of groceries at supermarkets. At first Richard resisted the advice. He had figured out one way of doing his grocery shopping, and it seemed easier to stick with something familiar rather than trying something new. But, ultimately, the logic of Patty's advice prevailed. Richard started taking a bus out to the Meijer store on the outskirts of town.

Tatzmann long believed that the key factor holding Richard back, aside from his illiteracy, was his partial deafness. The hearing loss wasn't diagnosed until the mid 1980s, when Tatzmann took Richard to the Michigan State University Audiology Department for an intensive workup. Doctors discovered that Richard suffered from two kinds of hearing loss: congenital and environmental. Examiners found that Richard had particular trouble distinguishing vowels, which at least partially explained his slurred speech and perhaps also shed some light on his reading difficulties.

The tests further revealed he had trouble hearing sounds above a certain range, and he could process words spoken by men much easier than those spoken by women. Richard already knew that. He often had difficulty understanding what women said. Embarrassed at having to continually ask women to repeat themselves, Richard often chose, instead, to remain oblivious to what they were saying. It was no wonder that he formed few attachments to women.

Shortly after the testing at MSU, Richard was fitted with a hearing aid, but it didn't work out. Never having developed the ability to tune out the peripheral noises of everyday life, Richard was overwhelmed by the flood of extraneous sounds that the defects in his hearing had blocked out all his life. He had trouble concentrating and was suffering chronic headaches. Eventually, he quit wearing the hearing aid.

He preferred missing some things over hearing too much.

At work, Richard had access to Babcock whenever he wanted it. Where Richard was concerned, Babcock had an open-door policy. This wasn't always convenient for Babcock. It wasn't so much that Richard kept the director from his work. Babcock had no qualms about showing Richard the door when he ran out of time for chitchat — and Richard never took offense at getting brushed off occasionally. It was more a matter of conscience. One of Babcock's continuous projects during those years was figuring out ways to trim the Mental Health budget. Richard seemed to be looking over Babcock's shoulder at every blow of the budget ax. And he was never the least bit shy in pointing out to his boss that the cuts were not in the best interests of the mental health consumers.

While Richard's input sometimes kept Babcock awake at night, the director knew that Richard was good for the Mental Health Department because, for one thing, he helped Babcock and his assistants resist the bureaucratic tendency to become detached from the concerns of the consumers. Holed up in their Lansing offices, staring at numbers and arguing over what was politically expedient, administrators had a tendency to lose sight of their true missions. One thing Richard brought to the process was a constant reality check. He had been on the receiving end of things. He knew how the policies formulated in Lansing played on the other side of the gate.

One Saturday, Babcock was speaking at a consumers meeting at Alma College. Richard was also at the meeting. Babcock offered Richard a ride back to Lansing. During the trip home, Babcock stopped to address a constituent's concern. The director had received a letter from a couple whose 10-year-old daughter was a resident in a state-run nursing home in Mt. Pleasant, an hour north of Lansing. The girl was severely disabled, both physically and mentally. The parents wanted to make sure their daughter was getting adequate care.

It happened to be an unseasonably warm day in early spring. Babcock, accompanied by Richard, walked into the nursing home in the late afternoon, when the outside temperature had climbed to 75 degrees. It was stifling inside the home. As the visitors walked down a hallway and into the girl's room, Richard mentioned to Babcock that the place was unbearably warm. It was more than a casual observation. Richard meant to imply that Babcock ought to do something about it before they left.

The director had to admit that, although he also had noticed the stuffiness of the place, the discomfort had registered with him only in an abstract way. He knew he would be in the home only briefly, so it didn't occur to him to try to improve the situation. Richard, on the other hand, put himself in the position of the residents. He insisted Babcock use his influence to get the staff to start the air-conditioning. The staff resisted at first, saying it was too early in the season for air-conditioning. Richard countered that the calendar had nothing to do with it, it was the comfort of the patients that mattered. Before they left, the air-conditioning units were humming.

Naturally, Richard used the time in the car to lobby the boss on the museum and the importance of giving him and Manfred Tatzmann the tools they needed to jump-start the effort. A Civil Service employee, Tatzmann had survived the Democratic takeover to become a permanent member of the Department of Mental Health.

By this time, of course, Tatzmann and Richard had become close friends. More than a friend, Tatzmann had become Richard's mentor. Tatzmann, in fact, had begun to accompany Richard on his various trips around the country, serving as travel agent, booking agent, tour guide and acting coach. Richard was capable of air travel on his own. He had proven that on his California trip. But it was extremely difficult for a person who couldn't read, especially when he had schedules to keep and arrangements to make.

Having somebody along with him made traveling a lot easier. In fact, Tatzmann tried to turn each trip into an educational experience for Richard. Tatzmann used the occasions to teach him, not only geography, but social science, history, nature and whatever happened to present itself along the road.

Fortunately for Richard, Babcock believed in the message Richard was delivering. He made allowances for the travel schedules of both Richard and Tatzmann, even though he knew that it sometimes created tension among the staff members who had to pick up the slack. But as Babcock saw it, Richard obviously was good for the image of the mental health system in Michigan and, in fact, was a goodwill ambassador for the state in general. Tatzmann went with Richard to the White House and just about every other place his mission took him.

If anybody was going to bring Richard's museum idea to fruition, Tatzmann was the likely candidate. With Babcock's blessing, Tatzmann took responsibility for reassessing the project, determining if there was any life left in it and, if so, reviving it. During their trips together, Tatzmann and Richard talked frequently about the declining enthusiasm for a full-blown museum. The practical objections to an actual building devoted to the historical artifacts of mental health were well documented. A building required heat and electricity. It demanded maintenance. It needed a staff. Who was going to pay for it all, and would it be money well spent?

But another factor, perhaps the most important one, was the question that some people saw as a gaping hole in the original committee's agenda. It was the question, they said, that should have been at the top of the list:

Who would visit a museum of mental health?

Although it might not have been politically correct to say so, a lot of people doubted there would be much interest in such an attraction. The Feasibility Committee had named Traverse City as the most likely site for the museum, at least partly because northwest Michigan had a substantial tourism base. Theoretically, those same tourists, in between bouts on the ski slopes, boat rides and trips to the Sleeping Bear Dunes, would stop to take in the sights of the museum.

In theory, it sounded good. But was it really a practical analysis? Were people on vacation likely to abandon the beaches of Lake Michigan, or the golf courses, so they could delve into the history of mental health in Michigan? With the exception of Richard, even the staunchest advocates of mental health reform had to admit, after all, it was a pretty dreary topic, especially since everybody agreed the exhibit should be educational and not simply a chamber of horrors with a collection of straitjackets and shackles and shock machines.

Maybe a museum was not the best way to go. Maybe there was a better way to get the word out. After all, you could build a church, but if nobody came to the services, what good would it do? However noble the message, it was worthless if not delivered. Maybe there was a lesson in Richard's missionary approach. Maybe it would make more sense to take the message to the people. Maybe what they needed was a traveling show.

As early as October 1981, Tatzmann was growing more and more convinced that the museum project had to go back to the drawing board for a fundamental reworking. He wrote to Mental Health director Babcock:

> I met with Mike Smith, museum curator from the Michigan Historical Commission on Oct. 21, 1981 to get a feel regarding the feasibility and practicality of a mental health museum. He was aware of some of the background work done ... and is acquainted with Richard.
>
> In discussing the concept, we agreed that a "museum" may not be the vehicle we are looking for. Rather, we are looking at an "educational exhibit," or "visitor's center." Either could fill the needs Richard saw without the drawbacks of having a full-fledged museum.... A mobile exhibit would allow us to go to the people, rather than have the people come to us. It would allow us to test the marketability of a mental health museum and would simultaneously be written off as an educational opportunity, thus opening doors to further funding.
>
> In discussing the funding aspect of such an exhibit, Mike expressed the belief that an "educational exhibit" is more likely to receive positive consideration from a

foundation or some other funding source than a museum. A museum implies bricks and mortar, which most funding sources tend to shy away from.

I have had an opportunity to discuss this idea with Richard and he is also quite excited about this being a practical way to go. I will continue to explore this issue and keep you informed.

Richard's dream to turn the former Coldwater administration building into a mental health museum had been modified by the original committee. Two years after that Fourth of July when the idea for a museum seized him, it was in the hands of another committee. There was just no way to avoid bureaucracy.

A month later, Tatzmann proposed the formation of a committee to study the traveling-exhibit idea. It would include Tatzmann and Richard, a representative of the governor's office, plus eight other Mental Health officials and private citizens. Former Governor Milliken agreed to be the honorary cochairman. So did Governor Blanchard and, later, Governor Engler. It met for the first time in February 1982. The committee voted to set up a nonprofit corporation to begin raising money for the exhibit.

Later that year, it became Mental Health Educational Exhibit Inc. Its purpose: "To establish and operate a traveling exhibit showing the historical progression of treatment and services for persons with mental illness and mental retardation in Michigan; and showing the services and advocacy provided by ... public and private agencies and to foster an increased awareness of the needs of persons with mental illness or mental retardation."

A press release went out from the Michigan Department of Mental Health: "A traveling mental health exhibit for Michigan moved a step closer to reality today with action to form a private non-profit corporation."

The committee adopted a slogan proposed by Richard: "Say Yes to Mental Health in Michigan." Richard bought a button-making machine and churned out buttons bearing the slogan. He sold them to just about everybody who crossed his path. The committee's original goal was to raise $50,000 — from private donations, foundations and business groups. That goal was later changed to $150,000. The committee also started rounding up moral support, in the form of testimonials from political leaders around the state:

I write to encourage the efforts of Richard Prangley and others to "Say Yes to Mental Health in Michigan." It is the goal of these persons to raise funds to create a series of mental health exhibits. These will be made available to schools and organizations.

I have met personally with Mr. Prangley. I am impressed by his dedication and vision. The work of Richard and his colleagues will do much to improve mental health.

I endorse this effort and encourage your support of it.

Terry McKane, mayor of Lansing

The Mental Health Educational Exhibit, Inc. is to be congratulated for its efforts to develop a means of educating the general public as to the truth about mental handicaps.

This area is one which has suffered from a great deal of misinformation and lack of understanding through the years. Your development of a traveling exhibit to help dispel the myths which surround the subject can be a very worthwhile contribution to an increased public understanding of this area.

I wish you every success as you develop the project in the coming months and years.

Coleman Young, mayor of Detroit

In November 1982, a private company from Midland called Design Craftsmen submitted a proposal to design the traveling exhibit. Design Craftsmen recommended a portable exhibit that could be transported in a specially fitted van to schools, churches, shopping malls, fairs, festivals and so on. It would include "photographic imagery, stimulating copy and creative graphic treatment and layout."

For the next three years, the project meandered along, without going anywhere, except in circles. The designer dragged his feet and, ultimately, quit. The committee lost its focus and drifted into a state of inertia.

Meanwhile, the traveling exhibit *behind* the traveling exhibit, Richard Prangley, continued to make an impression.

National News

President Reagan tried to turn the ceremony into politics. It's a good thing
I was there — to make sure it wasn't just politics.
                                                            — Richard Prangley

In 1983, Richard was invited to the White House. Three years into the decade, President Ronald Reagan was about to proclaim the 1980s the "Decade of the Disabled." The proclamation, issued on November 28, said, in part:

> During the 1981 International Year and the 1982 National Year of Disabled Persons, we learned about the many accomplishments of disabled persons, both young and old. We also gained vast new insights into the significant impact that access to education, rehabilitation, and employment have on their lives.
>
> The progress we have made is a tribute to the courage and determination of our disabled people, to innovative research and development both in technology and training techniques to assist the disabled, and, to those — whether in the private or public sectors — who have given so generously of their time and energies to help enrich the lives of disabled persons.
>
> Now, therefore, I, Ronald Reagan … do hereby proclaim the years 1983 through 1992 as the National Decade of Disabled Persons. I call upon all Americans … to join our continuing efforts to assist disabled people and to continue the progress made over the past two years.

Reagan's publicists knew he would get more mileage out of the proclamation if disabled people were actually involved in the ceremony. Two hundred handicapped people from throughout the United States were summoned to Washington in late November to witness the signing of the proclamation. Richard was among them, having been nominated for the honor by the Michigan Association for Retarded Citizens. Tatzmann went along. He drove from Lansing to D.C. and, as always, pointed out the points of interest along the way.

On the verge of his 34th birthday, Richard was ripe for the assignment. It seemed like a natural progression for him. Lobbying in the state capital or the nation's capital, it was essentially the same thing. He'd be pitching his message to a president instead of a governor. But the message was the same.

Richard imagined himself face-to-face, one-on-one, with Reagan. The prospect caused him no trepidation. In fact, it exhilarated him. He half expected to add Reagan to his list of friends in high places.

For Richard, this was the most formal occasion of his life, and, for the first time since 1971, the first day he went to his parents' home for dinner, he tried to put on a tie for the White House ceremony. But every time he tried to tighten the knot, he could feel the hands of the Coldwater attendant around his neck. He went to the White House wearing a turtleneck sweater and dress pants.

But even without a tie, Richard managed to make a splash during his brief stay in Washington. In fact his *lack* of a tie became national news. On the day Richard was in Washington, *USA Today* ran a "Newsmakers" feature on Richard, complete with a photo of him. By *USA Today* standards, the 12-inch treatment was positively in-depth. Under the headline, "He Speaks for the Mentally Slow," the story said, in part:

> When Richard Prangley, 33, dresses this morning for a meeting with President Reagan, he will not put on a tie. He has refused to wear one ever since an attendant at the state mental institution in Coldwater, Mich. used a tie in an attempt to strangle him. [Actually "refused" is not the right word. Richard would have liked nothing better than to wear a necktie to the White House. He simply couldn't tolerate it.]
>
> Such incidents were a part of Prangley's life from the age of 6, when his family had him committed due to his apparent mental retardation, to the age of 22, when it was determined that Prangley did not belong in an institution. His commitment to Coldwater was representative of the tendency in the 1950s to put mentally slow people in hospitals.

For the kicker to the story, Richard came up with another one of his million dollar quotes. Summarizing his journey from Coldwater to his appointment with the president, Richard said, "I've gone from the warehouse to the White House."

To Richard's dismay, he never got the opportunity that day to speak to Reagan directly. Too bad. He had a few things he wanted to tell the president and fully expected to deliver his message man to man. But after signing the proclamation, the president paused only long enough for a few photographs before leaving the room.

Determined to have his chat with the president, Richard asked an attendant if he could stop by the Oval Office later. Chuckling at Richard's naiveté, the attendant said the president was a little too busy for that sort of thing. Richard didn't get the joke.

Though disappointed, Richard wasn't entirely surprised by Reagan's quick exit. He had been around politicians long enough to know that sometimes they favored photo opportunities over substantive discussions. It was part of the game.

Richard didn't get Reagan's ear. He did, however, get the chance to address the nation. His charm and his readiness to speak up went over as well in the nation's capital as they had in the state capital. Richard was plucked from among the 200 people at the ceremony to do a live interview with David Hartman of *Good Morning, America.*

The show's producers, having seen the *USA Today* piece, tracked Richard and Tatzmann down at their hotel and asked Tatzmann if he and Richard would be willing to do an early-morning chat the following day. Richard didn't hesitate for a second. Again, it seemed to him like a natural progression: from Channel 10 in Lansing to *Good Morning, America.*

A limousine picked up Richard and Tatzmann the next morning and took them to the ABC studios. Both men got the makeup treatment before they when on camera. By then, Richard clearly was creeping toward middle age. His hairline was receding. His natural stockiness, combined with his fondness for food, was turning into the rotundness Richard would carry into his 40s and beyond. Not that it made him self-conscious. He happily answered Hartman's questions about his institutionalization and his vision of the future for the mentally disabled.

Hartman loved him. Richard's enthusiasm and sincerity played as well on national TV as it had in the local media. As Richard saw it, the opportunity to deliver his message to a national audience almost made up for his disappointment at not getting the president's ear. When it was all over, Richard matter-of-factly told reporters that his comments on *Good Morning, America* turned a ceremonial gesture into a legitimate advance for the disabled. "I didn't want [the proclamation] to be a political tool," Richard said. "My being there turned that around and put the focus on the disabled again."

The immediate focus, however, was on Richard. A few weeks after the Hartman interview aired, the New York City tabloid the *Star* ran a story under this four-column headline: "Scandal of 'Retarded' Man Wrongly Locked Up in Mental Home for 15 Years." Under the main headline this subhead appeared: "Brave battle for a normal life ends in triumph as he meets the president."

The *Star* quoted Richard extensively and put a soap-opera spin on his story:

A courageous crusade against the abuse of the retarded is being waged by a young man who spent 15 nightmarish years in a mental institution — where he was put by mistake.

And Richard Prangley, who was whisked away at the age of six because his learning disability was misdiagnosed as retardation, recently enjoyed his finest moment on the long road back to a normal life when he met President Reagan at the White House to speak on behalf of the mentally handicapped.

Of course, Richard *hadn't* met Reagan, but apparently the *Star* liked the other version of the story.

Here's how the *Star* described Richard's introduction to Cottage 41: "He was taken upstairs into a huge dormitory filled with boys who were all screaming and yelling. Some wore strait jackets. Several were severely mentally disturbed. A few were insane."

The *Star* reporter wasn't the only member of the journalism pack to be intrigued by the Hartman interview. The producers of CBS News also noticed. In early January 1984, a little more than a month after his appearance on *Good Morning, America* Richard reached the pinnacle of media exposure with first-class treatment on *Sunday Morning,* the CBS weekly news-feature show hosted by Charles Kurault. Correspondent Marlene Sanders reported the segment, called "A Reason to Be Bitter."

Obviously, the CBS people became impressed with Richard's story. The more they got to know him, the more they realized that the man was worth more than 30 seconds. What started out as a brief interview for a light treatment quickly developed into an 11-minute segment. The more Sanders heard, the more she saw the Richard Prangley story as a full-blown news feature. She and the camera crew ended up spending two days in Michigan, filming both in Lansing and Coldwater. This was no sound bite. This was in-depth treatment on one of the most respected news shows of the day.

Kurault, perched on his famous stool, opened the segment this way: "Marlene Sanders has a story to tell now. It is a story of an injustice, but it is much more than that. It is the story of a man who rose above injustice. And forgave it. And made himself whole."

Like *Readin' and Writin' Ain't Everything,* the *Sunday Morning* segment began with shots of the foreboding brick facades of the buildings at Coldwater. Shot in winter, the buildings looked all the more unfriendly.

Sanders started: "These dreary buildings are part of the Coldwater, Michigan, State Home for the Retarded. Thousands of people spent their entire lives here."

The next scene showed Sanders and a particularly well-groomed Richard walking among the rubble inside the abandoned Cottage 41, which was soon to be demolished. It was a difficult day for Richard. He didn't mind going to Coldwater, but would have preferred to do the shooting at the marker he helped dedicate in 1981. He proposed that, but Sanders wanted to shoot inside the dayroom of Cottage 41. Richard swallowed hard and agreed to confront the ghosts of his youth. If that's what it took to get a national audience, that's what he would do. As Richard stepped into the room, a flood of bad memories washed over him. The discomfort showed in his face; he looked terrified.

Standing next to Richard, Sanders asked, "Without the people in it, does it seem like the same place?"

Richard replied, "It brings back memories."

Sanders: "You can picture them all."

Richard, much more subdued than normal: "Yeah."

Then Sanders talked directly to the camera. "Richard Prangley lived here for 16 years. It was a 16-year mistake."

Actually it was 15, but in the very earliest newspaper stories, the figure 16 was used, and the mistake kept getting repeated. Richard himself thought he had been inside Coldwater for 16 years, until somebody from the Michigan Department of Mental Health actually checked his records and found he had been there from June 1956 until May 1971.

Sanders then asked Richard what bothered him about coming back to Cottage 41.

Richard, still very subdued, replied: "Well, just being here. You know, I'm trying to leave this all behind me."

The camera crew followed Richard as he made his rounds delivering mail in the Michigan Department of Mental Health. He was shown participating in work-related conversations as well as social chitchat.

Sanders: "He's 34 years old. He was born prematurely. Learning disabilities, complicated by defects in hearing and sight, caused him to be put into a state home for the mentally retarded when he was 6 years old. He was not retarded."

Actually this may be going too far. Although "retarded" is an imprecise term, some aspects of Richard's development did, indeed, lag behind the norm. It's likely he suffered brain damage at birth.

Sanders continued: "The institution was his home for 16 years until doctors discovered he didn't belong there."

Again, that was shortcut journalism. It's not like Richard was sprung from the institution like a convict suddenly freed by somebody else's confession. There was no revelation that led to Richard's freedom. He worked his way out of Coldwater. Nobody "discovered" that he didn't belong there.

By the time the *Sunday Morning* segment was filmed, Richard was deep into his role as reformer and advocate. He described this mission for CBS. The segment also showed the Coldwater institution as it was in 1984 — in Sanders words, "comfortable, clean and humane."

Sanders: "In 1956, when Richard was committed, it was crowded — a warehouse for the discarded. Remote from society — out of sight, as well as out of mind."

Again, Richard and Sanders stood in the Cottage 41 dayroom.

Sanders: "What did you do here when you were 6 years old? How did you spend your days?"

Richard: "A lot of people were laying around — sitting on the benches all day."

Sanders summarized Richard's life after his release from Coldwater, then introduced Tatzmann as a "special friend" — "a kind of parent Richard never had."

Tatzmann: "I started inquiring about his story and how he got to be in the department. The unit I was working in at that time had oversight over many activities in the department. He and I struck up a friendship. The more I got to know him, the more I got to like him. I wanted to be his friend."

To make the point that Richard had been able to cultivate "more powerful people," there was a shot of a photo of him and former Gov. William Milliken.

The segment then showed Richard at the home of Pat Babcock, who had replaced Ochberg as head of the department. Sanders said, "Richard is a frequent visitor at the home of Patrick Babcock, director of the Michigan Department of Mental Health."

Years later, Babcock recalled that the CBS crew insisted he rearrange the furniture in his family room so he would be sitting against a background of books, looking scholarly. On camera, Babcock said: "The real story of Richard and the many thousands of people like Richard is the potential contribution that those individuals can make if given a chance. It's a story of courage, frankly; courage to change one's life. We really are moving against a history of exclusion to one of involving people in the mainstream of society, and I just hope we never fall back to a situation where we isolate people because they're a little different."

The segment also showed Richard with Patricia Babcock, the director's wife. They were sitting at a table at the Babcock house. She was laboring with flash cards, trying to teach Richard how to read.

Sanders asked Richard how it felt to be learning how to read. Richard said, "It makes me feel gorgeous."

Sanders: "Considering what you went through, you seem like a pretty happy, well-adjusted person. How come?"

Richard answered the question by saying he tried not to be bitter. He wanted to "go forward."

Then Sanders delved into a touchy subject: Richard's relationship with his parents.

"One of the things Richard has had to put behind him is his feeling toward his parents," she said. "They had committed him to Coldwater on the advice of doctors, who had misdiagnosed his condition. But he knows they meant well, and since they live in a nearby town, he is seeing them again and has come to terms with the past."

Ironically, although CBS called the segment "A Reason to Be Bitter," it closed with Richard saying, "There's no reason to be bitter."

The story drew rave reviews. Viewers particularly liked the fact that Richard carried no grudges. Virtually every letter applauded his lack of rancor. Some of the letters were addressed directly to Richard, in care of the Michigan Department of Mental Health:

From Panorama City, California:

I saw you on *Sunday Morning.* Your spectacular attitude made me feel so good. You are a most genuine person and deserve the highest praise. How I wish there were more people like you around. Seldom do I ever use the word "superior," but in your case it's applicable. You're a superior person. All the best to you. Good health and happiness always.

From Irving, Texas:

I was deeply touched by your story. I think you're a very sincere and loving person to have such a wonderful outlook on life. Your attitude about life and work and not looking back to the past, but towards the future, was an inspiration to me.... You definitely make a difference.

From Waltham, Massachusetts:

After listening to you ... I have found more courage and strength than I've had in a long time. I will look harder for the sunshine in my life. I am writing mostly to let you know you are a beautiful person and I have unlimited respect and admiration for you.

From Minneapolis–St. Paul Minnesota:

I am your age and in trying to put myself into your story, I'm afraid I may not have kept the faith in life that you so clearly have kept. Your capacity to forgive can only be rivaled by Jesus. And on this Sunday morning, your words of love have brought us much closer to the heart of God than all the sermons by holy men.... You have much to say that the world needs to hear. You're a gorgeous person.

From Princeton, New Jersey:

For someone to want to forgive and forget all of the terrible things that happened to you for 15 years while you were in the institution really does take a special person. We all need to be more like you — less selfish and more forgiving.

From Plattsburgh, New York:

You are not alone. I, too, know the futility of isolation, and I wholly agree with your philosophy of going forward. Many who have not experienced what you have live in cages of their own design. Let us hope they too become free.

In 1985, CBS reran the *Sunday Morning* episode and provided an update. In a letter dated Oct. 10, 1985, Tatzmann wrote to Bill Moran, the *Sunday Morning* producer:

Dear Bill:

I thought you and others at CBS who made the decision to rerun the program on Richard would like to know the fantastic impact this story, again, has had on people all over the country. The attached letters are just some of the ones received from every corner of the country. Clearly, the story is a rare one, which impacts all who see it.

Thank you for having the faith in us by continuing to follow Richard's story. He has now developed a mini-museum in his basement and is fighting with the State to allow him to have artifacts for his museum. Meanwhile, he keeps pursuing his dreams of having a Mental Health Exhibit and having his life's story put into print or film.

Forgive and Forget

I thought if I could show my parents that I wasn't wild anymore, they would accept me. I thought I could show them, by my behavior, that I was a different person. I don't know — maybe it was too late.

— Richard Prangley

"No reason to be bitter." "Forgive and forget." "Put the past behind and go forward." Richard used those phrases and others like them all the time. They were his mantras, his passwords through so many doors as he navigated life on the outside. They allowed him to maneuver. The politicians and bureaucrats liked to hear those conciliatory words. So did the reporters and bosses and award presenters. About Richard Prangley it was often said that, despite the fact he had been locked up for 15 years unnecessarily, despite the fact he received no education and very little love, he wasn't bitter. Not Richard.

That was part of what made him special. That was part of what made him appealing. Nobody, it seemed, wanted to listen to another bitter victim of injustice. Richard, on the other hand, was a victim of injustice, all right, but he wasn't blaming anybody. He wasn't looking for revenge. He didn't go around saying "poor me" all the time. The man was upbeat.

How did he do it? How was he able to forgive and forget that he was robbed of 15 years of his life — 15 years that were gone forever?

Actually, he wasn't. Richard wasn't being dishonest when he told people that he was trying to put the past behind him and concentrate on the future. He really was. He knew that was a crucial part of his plan for a productive life. He knew what happened to the ex-Coldwater residents who dwelt on the past, who refused to get on with their lives. They ended up back in the institution or living on the street or in jail. As for his frequent denials of bitterness, Richard was trying very hard to keep it off the front burner, but it was there, simmering.

CBS correspondent Marlene Sanders said Richard was seeing his parents again and he had come to terms with the past. No doubt that was what Richard told her. That's what she wanted to hear because she knew it was what the view-

ers wanted to hear. Richard's 15 wasted years made a good story, and his conciliatory attitude always made it even better. Suffering. Forgiveness. Reconciliation. It was a definite crowd-pleaser. It was what Richard himself wanted to
believe, and sometimes he could even convince himself that it was so.

But the truth was that Richard was deeply troubled by the fact that his relationship with his parents and siblings had progressed hardly at all since that awkward, painful conversation Richard had with his mother the day he walked out
of the institution. That was the day he could hardly wait to get his hands on a
telephone so he could impress his parents with the news he was free and arrange
the reunion he had yearned for for so long.

From Richard's point of view, it was that simple. Sure, he had some questions about what his parents had done. He wanted an explanation. He wanted
to sit down with his parents and hash things out. Maybe after he heard what
they had to say and after he got some things off his chest, they could move on.
Nobody could erase what had happened, but maybe they could get past it.

But for John and Dorothy Prangley, it was much more complicated. Over
the 15 years Richard was in Coldwater, the Prangleys had gradually disengaged
from their son. Evidently, they had managed to convince themselves that
Richard was where he belonged — that his separation from the family was in
the family's best interests and, ultimately, in Richard's best interests.

They did, after all, have the other children to think about. It's not like they
hadn't tried. For six years, they had tried to manage Richard and couldn't. They
had done their best. Of course, Richard never understood that. When John and
Dorothy drove to Coldwater to visit their son, all he did was beg them to take
him home — or repeat those hard-to-believe stories about the terrible things
that were happening to him there.

The visits didn't seem to do Richard any good, and they certainly didn't
make life easier for the Prangleys. Maybe, they ultimately concluded, it would
be easier on everybody if they just stayed away, if they just detached themselves
from their son. They tried it. For weeks at a time, they stayed away. It wasn't that
difficult. They told themselves it probably was better for Richard, too. Gradually, the time between visits grew longer and longer, from weeks, to months, to
years. They sent birthday and Christmas cards. They signed permission forms
when Richard needed medical treatment. They were informed of his progress.
He was still their son. Life went on.

Richard's release from the institution changed everything. Suddenly he was
no longer a person to be visited or not visited, like a distant relative in the hospital on an extended stay. Suddenly, Richard was capable of taking the initiative
and seeking out the Prangleys. But John and Dorothy were so far into their
detachment it was impossible for them to just suddenly reverse the process. For
the past 15 years, they had been operating on certain assumptions. They had

adjusted their lives in a certain way. Now they were being asked to accept a whole different reality.

In his more candid moments years after he got out of Coldwater, Richard, struggling to understand why he couldn't get any closer to his parents than he did, came to a startling realization: His parents, whether consciously or not, had expected him to be in the institution for the rest of his life, certainly for the rest of their lives, and had slowly erased him from their family. It was almost as though Richard had died. That's why his sudden reappearance at their doorstep left them disoriented and confused.

There was more to it than the unexpected reemergence of somebody the Prangleys almost had managed to forget. Richard's release reopened old sores. The fact was that if Richard had been deemed ultimately unreleasable, his parents would have been vindicated in their decision to put him there when he was 6. Instead, he got out. The more Richard thought about it, the more it seemed to him that his life beyond the institution raised uncomfortable questions — questions his parents didn't want to think about.

Could he have been released earlier? Should they have done something to bring that about? And the most troubling question of all: Should he have been there in the first place? Richard came to believe that his parents had adopted a strategy to cope with the fact that they had a son inside an institution. Richard's phone call in 1971 upset that strategy. Thirteen years later, they still were trying to figure out a new one.

As for Richard's 10 siblings, no real bonds had been formed in the first place. They all knew about Richard, in a vague sense; some of the older ones had gone with their parents to pick him up at Cottage 41 and take him to lunch or dinner. Sometimes they'd stop at a playground, where Richard, even as a teenager, would behave like a 5-year-old. Sometimes there would be other people around; it was embarrassing.

One way or another, it was always an unpleasant, unsettling, emotionally draining experience, one that left their parents distant and unhappy. It was always the same. Richard always behaved badly, talking too loudly, knocking over his glass of milk and causing people in the restaurant to stare. He always begged to go home and demanded to know why he couldn't go. When that didn't work, he would start telling wild stories about life inside the institution and about the horrible things the attendants were doing to him. The lunches and dinners would grind along to their inevitable conclusions: with Richard crying and thrashing about and Mom and Dad looking miserable.

On the way back home, John and Dorothy always assured their children that Richard had been exaggerating about his treatment in the institution. They explained, each time, why it was best for everybody that Richard remain where he was. It was what the doctors recommended; it was what everybody recommended. Soon the Prangley family would be home again — settled back into the life they knew, the life without Richard. He was like a distant cousin in prison — locked up for good reasons.

And then, suddenly, having served his time, he was released. One day he was out of sight and out of mind; the next day he was back in town, claiming a place in the family, expecting to take up where he had left off.

And why wouldn't he expect that? For Richard, time stopped, in a sense, on June 4, 1956, the day he ceased to become a member of the Prangley family. He would be a part of the family again someday; he never quite got over believing that. He spent 15 years waiting to step back into his role as son and brother. But for the other Prangleys, time kept moving; they left Richard behind.

Between the time Richard left Grand Rapids and the time he got settled in Lansing, there was very little contact between Richard and his family. However, John and Dorothy Prangley, as well as Richard's brothers and sisters, couldn't help but notice the publicity Richard was getting. At first it was strictly local, but the scope quickly broadened. It became impossible to ignore.

People started asking questions. Those who knew that Richard was a member of the Prangley family were curious about these new developments. Was it true? Was Richard a lot smarter than everyone thought? Had the institution made such a profound difference in Richard, or had the intelligence been there all along? Those who didn't know were always asking Richard's parents and siblings if they were related to the man in the newspaper. Prangley wasn't a common name.

The newspapers and television and radio stations were calling this guy a "phenomenon," a throwaway kid who survived his exile and was now hobnobbing with governors. He was coming up with ideas worthy of study by committees, and even serving on those committees. Everybody was calling him a victim of a tragic mistake, saying he never should have been put in the place where John and Dorothy Prangley put him.

Sometimes the reporters called the Prangleys and asked personal questions about why they did this, or why they didn't do that. John and Dorothy always refused to answer the questions. It was nobody's business. The reporters could write what they wanted; they would, anyway. John and Dorothy refused to be put in the position of defending a decision they made 20 years earlier, a decision for which they sought counsel. They weren't about to be second guessed, certainly not by reporters who knew nothing about what the Prangleys had gone through. They were naturally tight-lipped people, and the assault from reporters only strengthened their resolve to keep their family's business to themselves.

But it wasn't just the reporters who were saying John and Dorothy Prangley gravely underestimated their son. The experts were lining up to get on the bandwagon; everybody was saying that Richard probably would have been OK with a little special help. Where were those experts when Richard was turning the Prangley household upside down? Where were they when John and Dorothy Prangley were facing those hard decisions? How come the experts saw the situation so differently in 1956?

The way some of the stories made it sound, John and Dorothy Prangley were ignorant, careless people who dumped their son in Coldwater just because he had been a rambunctious baby. The stories made it sound like the Prangleys were bad parents who didn't care about their son, the kind of people who would leave a baby on a doorstep.

The children of John and Dorothy knew their parents were good people, and they began to resent the implications. Naturally, they circled their wagons around their parents. They went on the defensive. Why was Richard doing this to his parents? Why was he so insistent on dredging up the past? Didn't he realize they already felt bad and that this only made them feel worse?

Ironically, he didn't. From Richard's point of view, the way back into his parents' hearts was in proving his competence. It was perfectly logical. They removed him from his home and family because he was incompetent and he didn't know how to function in society. So maybe the road back was to show them he was a valued human being; so valued, in fact, he made the newspapers and television news shows. He had ideas. He had friends in high places. He was more than competent; he was practically famous. Surely his parents would love him if he were famous. And didn't he always make it a point to tell the reporters he wasn't bitter, that he harbored no ill will against his parents?

Yet, the more Richard succeeded — the more he exploited the potential he wasn't supposed to possess, the more he proved he never belonged in Coldwater in the first place — the worse his parents' decision looked.

The adult Richard was, after all, the same person who went into the institution. Nobody could deny that. And nobody could deny that, despite what the doctors said in 1956, he was capable of learning. And yet he received no education, certainly not in the usual sense of the word, while he was at Coldwater. So he became a walking indictment of an unfortunate decision, a living, breathing accusation. And he was a phenomenon. He had the ear of the press.

From the point of view of his siblings, Richard talked out of both sides of his mouth. He was always going on about wanting to get close to his parents and siblings; he kept saying he wanted to become a real part of the family again. At the same time, he was constantly cooperating with the newspaper and television reporters who seemed intent on portraying his parents as uncaring monsters.

More than merely cooperating, Richard seemed to be actually initiating the stories. He could stop it any time; he could refuse to give interviews whenever he wanted to. He just didn't want to. He liked the attention. Maybe it was his way of getting even with his parents. Maybe he really was bitter, and ingenious, too, in a perverse sort of way.

On the rare occasions Richard saw his siblings, they often remarked sardonically on the publicity he was receiving and the high-powered company he was keeping. Richard couldn't figure out whether it was envy or just plain resentment. In any case, he couldn't help taking the bait, offering full-blown updates on the important things he was doing and the important people he knew on a first-name basis. Richard's brothers and sisters winked at each other. The general sentiment among them was that he was making most of it up or, at the very least, exaggerating about everything.

That was Richard, they told each other. He took everything to extremes. He couldn't have just a few ducks; he had to have 200 of them. He couldn't have just one collection; he had to have a dozen of them. He couldn't just have friends; he had to have famous, powerful friends. He couldn't just have a life; he had to have a mission. Weary of his bragging, some of the siblings liked to needle Richard by asking him if he had been elected governor yet. Richard had a standard answer for that one. He told them that he wasn't particularly interested in that job.

All of it — the publicity, the implications that a mistake had been made, and even Richard's success and triumphs — combined to insure that the gulf remained between him and his family. After all, he could not talk about his success without putting them in the context of his life at Coldwater. Kurault said that by learning to forgive, Richard "had made himself whole," but in fact a piece of him was missing. After 25 years of trying to go home, Richard still had a long way to go. Always, he would be trying to figure out the way home.

While Richard's relationship with his family was stalled, his public life continued to soar. After the David Hartman interview and the *Sunday Morning* episode, Richard was no longer strictly a Michigan phenomenon; he was national news. Richard began getting invitations to do talk shows all over the country. His first month of 1984 shaped up like this:

Jan. 19: "Pittsburgh 2 Day," Pittsburgh.
Jan. 20: "People Are Talking," Baltimore.
Jan. 23: "People Are Talking," Boston.
Feb. 2: "People Are Talking," San Francisco.

Tatzmann accompanied Richard on the four-city tour and shared the spotlight with him. Invariably, they sat side-by-side on a couch, Richard in a tan vested suit, a powder-blue turtleneck and a "Say Yes to Mental Health" button on his lapel, answering questions from the host, the studio audience and the call-ins.

Sometimes Richard and Tatzmann were joined by local mental health professionals — experts in deinstitutionalization or learning disabilities. But clearly, Richard was the star of the show.

The questions were predictable:

"What was it like in the institution?"

"What abuses did you suffer there?"

"Did you ever try to escape? Commit suicide?"

"Why did your parents put you there? Are they full of guilt today?"

"Are you bitter about what happened?"

Every time, Richard performed beautifully, gathering steam as he went along. He had heard all the questions before and never seemed to grow tired of answering them. He took each host down the curved road to Coldwater, into the urine-soaked dayroom. He told them about the physical and emotional abuse at the hands of the guards.

Unflinchingly, Richard provided the gory details when called upon to do so. And, with a sincerity that brought a hush to the studio, expressed his hopes for familial reconciliation.

In every town, Richard was Richard. And although he answered the same questions over and over again, he never had to worry about making his stories consistent. The truth was the truth.

After that, Richard spoke at conferences and participated in panel discussions. He gave after-dinner speeches. He offered advice and encouragement to those involved in creating independent-living opportunities for the mentally disabled.

In November, Richard accepted the first annual Bill Sackter Award, given each year to the person who best symbolizes independence for the mentally impaired. The presentation was made during a banquet at the 35th annual convention of the National Association for Retarded Citizens at the Opryland Hotel in Nashville. It marked the first time in the association's history that a major national award was given to a person who was mentally disabled. Richard's life story paralleled the man after whom the award was named. Bill Sackter was a Minnesota man who spent 44 years inside an institution before being released to a life of independence.

Sackter's story was made famous by the 1981 movie *Bill* and the sequel, *Bill: On His Own*. Mickey Rooney played the lead role in both films. An employee of the University of Iowa's School of Social Work, Sackter also became an ambassador and advocate for the mentally disabled and an inspiring role model for people with mental retardation. He died at age 70 on June 16, 1983.

The press release announcing the award began by describing Richard's return to Cottage 41 with the CBS film crew for the *Sunday Morning* episode: "The car wound its way down an all-but-deserted road and Richard Prangley, 34, stared out the window at his past. 'I can remember my mom and dad driving down this road when they brought me here,' he said. 'That was a long time ago.'"

The press release went on to explain why Prangley was chosen for the award: "In the 1980s the ARC has deepened its commitment toward encouraging and supporting the movement of people out of institutions and into community living settings, their rightful environment for achieving their greatest potential — and for enjoying life."

The previous year, ARC announced it would accept nominations for the award and drew hundreds of them from all over the country.

In nominating Prangley, ARC/Michigan President Kenneth Grounds wrote: "Reading Richard's life is like participating in a true-life adventure story. Certainly, Horatio Alger encountered fewer and less severe barriers than did Richard."

Rooney was there to present the award to Richard. Richard was asked what kind of a guy Rooney was. Richard said, "Short — and funny."

Richard received a letter from Gov. James Blanchard:

> I would like to add to your many commendations by extending my congratulations and best wishes for your recent selection as the recipient of the 1984 Bill Sackter Award.
>
> Richard, you certainly have been a very strong advocate and supporter for the rights and services to mental health patients. Your involvement has gone above and beyond the call of duty and you serve as a source of inspiration to the many who know you.
>
> On behalf of my staff, Richard, please accept our congratulations and wishes for continued good health, happiness and peace.

ARC was so taken with Richard that leaders of the organization invited him to address the ARC national convention in Wichita, Kansas, the following year. It was another first for Richard: the first time a person with a mental disability had been chosen to be the keynote speaker at an ARC convention. Richard couldn't use a written speech, or even notes, because he couldn't read. He stepped to the podium the evening of April 12, 1985 and spoke extemporaneously — "from the heart," as he described it. Richard's delivery was so moving it brought many members of the audience to tears. The speech was recorded and, later, a friend of Richard's transcribed it. It filled 12 pages.

He started: "Last November I received the Bill Sackter Award. This award was not only an honor, but was a light beam, an example for others. I want to set an example for people who have similar backgrounds and are trying to rise above institutionalization. That is the reward for me, to give an example to other people and give them a chance. What you can do when you're given a chance! That's my award. It says I love people and I love to see others lifted up as well."

Richard spun the story of his life for the crowd, from his premature birth, to his role as an advocate, weaving in his personal philosophy: "There is a reason why some people are different. God put us here for a reason." Richard's rea-

son: to demonstrate, by what he did and what he said, the tragedy of under
estimating human potential.

Richard told the audience that someday a book would be written about his
life. He even had a title in mind: *From the Warehouse to the White House.* Later,
Richard became a member of the Michigan ARC.

One month later, Richard was giving another speech; this time it was back
in Lansing, on the steps of the Capitol. Richard organized a rally to mark Michigan's 125th year of providing public mental health services. Ever mindful of the
television cameras, Richard constructed a mock door — the symbolic "new door
to mental health." He walked through it with Pat Babcock, the new Mental
Health director, and James Blanchard, the new governor. The supporting characters came and went; Richard was always there, driving home his message.

That day on the steps of the Capitol, Richard also rang the "freedom bell,"
cast 31 years earlier from shackles and chains commonly used in earlier decades
to restrain mental patients. Richard also collected several commendations that
day. A photo of him standing beside Blanchard and Babcock was prominently
displayed in the *State Journal.*

As always, Richard was Exhibit A in the case for giving the mentally disabled a chance to fulfill their potential.

As for the nonliving exhibit, it continued to languish. In February 1985,
Tatzman transferred from Lansing to Marquette, in Michigan's upper peninsula.
The job of area director of Mental Health in the Upper Peninsula opened up,
and Tatzmann thought the move would be good for him and his family. The
move had little effect on his involvement with the traveling exhibit project, or
his relationship with Richard. Tatzman made frequent trips back to Lansing and
continued to be the main thrust, aside from Richard, behind the exhibit. Tatzmann was, however, dismayed by the inertia that had seized the project. In a
Sept. 5, 1985 letter to board members, Tatzmann expressed his frustration at the
lack of progress: "We can go no further until we, as a board, know what we are
looking for, i.e., philosophically, structurally and what impact. Therefore, we
have agreed to hold an all-day working session on Oct. 7, 1985."

Tatzmann outlined the specific questions to be addressed:

> What do we want to see in an exhibit, immediately and in the future?
> What story should it convey?
> What do we want it to accomplish?
> Where do we seek funding?
> How do we develop a plan to implement the above?

Clearly, Tatzmann had had enough dillydallying. Sounding like a frustrated
teacher, he admonished the board members: "We should not leave without con-

crete answers to all of the above. Over the past three years, all of these questions have been discussed (repeatedly), but we, as a board, have not committed ourselves to a single plan, concept or idea. We must now act to fulfill the expectations of those who have supported us to date.... We must act now to decisively move ahead and no longer vacillate."

But apparently Tatzmann's admonishment had little effect. Minutes of an Oct. 7, 1985 meeting of the Mental Health Educational Exhibit Board show that the discussion was not much different than it was in 1982.

The topics of discussion for that meeting, as recorded in the minutes:

1. What is the nature of the traveling exhibit.... Must be a dignified exhibit, not tacky and patched.... One permanent exhibit, plus one traveling exhibit.
2. Transporting the exhibit: Full-time driver too expensive ... should fit into a station wagon.
3. There was $2,000 in the account.

And so on. Would the exhibit ever become a reality?

Richard himself was losing patience. In a letter to the committee dated Oct. 7, 1985, the day of the above-mentioned meeting, Richard, with the help of a friend, put his thoughts in writing: "Where are we going with this mental health education movement? What does it take to pursue a project such as this?"

For the Jan. 20, 1986 board meeting, there was a lack of a quorum. There was also no quorum at the following meeting on April 15.

With a tenacity that sometimes appeared to be beyond all reason, Tatzmann plugged on. In a letter to the superintendent of the Michigan Department of Education dated Oct. 20, 1986, Tatzmann reported that the Department of Mental Health had provided Michigan Mental Health Education Exhibit Inc. a grant of $50,000 to put the exhibit together as part of Michigan's sesquicentennial celebration in 1987. In the letter, Tatzmann asked for a grant from the Department of Education.

Looking for more professional help in getting the project off the ground, the committee turned to the Impression 5 Science Museum in Lansing.

On Nov. 5, 1986, Tatzmann wrote a letter to Robert Russell, executive director of the museum, outlining the deal:

> Impression 5 will hire the necessary consultants, including a project coordinator. Our goal is to have a project coordinator in place by the end of November or early December. This individual will oversee the design and production of the exhibit, which will consist of 3 stages: Research and thematic development; design, including visuals and model plans; and fabrication. The time-line for completing this project consists of a May deadline to coincide with Mental Health Week. At

that time we hope to have a working prototype, with a more finalized product done in time for the Mental Health Convention in June.

Impression 5's exhibit would consist of 10 to 15 graphic panels, video disks, four hands-on activities and, finally, two computer stations, which would ultimately transform the project into something unforeseen at the time. The cost for the initial setup would be $78,500. It would be a classroom-size exhibit that could be folded up and packed into a van that would haul it to schools and community centers around the state. Impression 5 also offered to handle shipping and scheduling of the traveling museum for the first three years, at a cost of about $15,000 per year.

The committee had the plans for the exhibit. Now all it had to do was find somebody to build it and, of course, figure out a way to pay for it. The committee launched a massive campaign to raise the money. Richard sold his buttons. Tatzmann ran a marathon. Two marathons, actually; one on his feet and one on his computer keyboard. Tatzmann collected 173 rejection letters from foundations throughout the country. Even so, the committee raised enough money to start building the exhibit.

But the committee members had to wonder: Was last week's plan still valid this week? This was in the mid-1980s, when the world was on the verge of recasting itself in terms of interactive computer software.

As Tatzmann and the others started thinking about how the various pieces of the exhibit would go together, they began to realize the main thrust of the exhibit, the educational elements, could be written into a program for a Macintosh computer. It was the first step in a dramatic evolution of the project. By the time it was over, the project would bear little resemblance to the original concept.

Friends in High Places

I want to educate people. That's my goal. I want to show them that people with developmental disabilities are human beings, too. They have rights, too. And they have something to contribute to society.

— Richard Prangley

In January 1987, Babcock left the Mental Health Department to take over the state Department of Social Services. Not that it ended his association with Richard. Babcock often said — again, only half jokingly — that Richard saw his boss's ascension to Social Services, with its $6 billion annual budget, as merely another opportunity.

Not willing to accept the concept of compartmentalized spending, Richard never stopped trying to persuade his former boss to find some money in the Social Services cookie jar to help pay for the mental health exhibit. And it didn't end there. Babcock eventually left state government for a job at the Kellogg Foundation in Battle Creek. At the time, Richard didn't even know what a foundation was, but he quickly learned:

It was another source of money.

Babcock's chief deputy, Thomas Watkins Jr., took over as Mental Health director. Watkins brought front-line experience to the job. Before joining state government, he worked in four different mental health centers. Babcock had hired him as a deputy in 1983.

Again, Richard didn't waste any time bemoaning the fact that a personal friend of his was no longer calling the shots in the department. He simply went about the task of cultivating a new friend. Once again, the director's office had a new occupant. Richard didn't let that fact interfere with his natural right of access. From the start, he began easing his way into the new guy's office. And again, Richard found somebody who not only respected and supported what he was doing for himself and others, but also liked him. Whenever he could, Watkins listened to what Richard had to say.

Watkins was continually struck by the fact that Richard's inability to grasp the subtle, and sometimes irrelevant, complexities of issues often served the department well. The man had a way of reducing an issue to its basic elements: black or white; right or wrong; good for mental health consumers or bad for them. Watkins found Richard's relentless simplifications both maddening and enlightening.

The director and the other administrators were forced to wrestle with priorities and compromises. They had to decide what programs must be cut or altered or eliminated in the context of the resources available and the political landscape. Richard, on the other hand, had the luxury of looking at things strictly in terms of what was best for the people whose lives were affected by the decisions.

Once he had a foot in the door, Richard was never shy about slipping into Watkins' office unannounced and pointing out how much mental health consumers relied on this or that. He would hear a rumor about an anticipated cut in one program or another. He'd approach Watkins like a parent trying to get a wayward child back on track by appealing to his best instincts. He'd say to his boss: "You're not *really* thinking about doing that, are you?" Watkins couldn't always refrain from carrying out his intentions, but Richard was always there to insure that the director explored his actions from every perspective.

It wasn't always Richard seeking out the boss. Sometime Watkins would spot Richard in the cafeteria, eating his lunch alone, and would take the opportunity to sit down at Richard's table and bounce an idea or two off him. And, occasionally, Watkins accepted Richard's invitations to his flat, where he drank the tea Richard brewed and allowed himself to be advised and cajoled and persuaded.

Watkins described Richard as "a constant drum beat that strengthened my resolve to do the right thing." Richard's solutions to Watkins' problems often were too simplistic, but they were always motivated by the desire to do good.

Although Watkins' inclinations toward the deinstitutionalization of the mentally ill and developmentally disabled preceded his association with Richard, those sentiments only deepened under the tutelage of somebody who was, by all accounts, a walking indictment of indiscriminate institutionalization.

Watkins always saw Richard as a symbol of the human potential that had been wasting away behind the walls of places like the Coldwater State Home and Training Center. In a lengthy guest column Watkins wrote for the *Lansing State Journal's* op-ed page in September 1989, he outlined his plans for an "anti-stigma conference" that fall and specifically referred to Richard's traveling exhibit project, which, as Watkins put it, "addresses the potential of persons with mental illness and developmental disabilities."

Watkins, sounding like a more-eloquent Richard, wrote: "Thousands across Michigan, previously entombed in institutions for many years, are now able to lead normalized lives in the community. Not only are they capable of community living, but we now know that with the proper supports, they can hold jobs and be contributing members of the community."

When Watkins left the department, he asked that his employees refrain from buying him a going-away gift and, instead, pass the hat on behalf of Richard's traveling exhibit. They collected $2,200.

Like any department director, Watkins received many tokens of appreciation during his time in state government. Nearly all of them ended up in boxes that got moved from one place to another without ever getting unpacked. But Watkins always made it a point to seek out a simple wooden plaque he received from Richard for his support of the traveling exhibit project.

"Richard was as close to a saint as I'll ever come," Watkins once said. "If what happened to Richard happened to me, I'm afraid I would have been embittered for several lifetimes."

But Richard didn't have time for bitterness. The demands of an independent life left little room for brooding over past injustices.

In April 1990, the *Detroit Free Press* once again gave Richard first-class treatment. The spread consumed nearly two full pages in the paper's Sunday "Comment" section and featured six photographs: Richard at work; Richard at Clara's; Richard with his ducks ...

Under the headline "Crusade Against a Stigma," writer Patricia Chargot provided a complete workup on the man who was out to change the world. Collecting impressions of Richard from the people who knew him best, Chargot reached all the way back to members of the Detroit Film Collective, which had disbanded in the years following the production of *Readin' and Writin' Ain't Everything*. Chargot wrote:

> Countless friends and admirers — including a former Michigan governor, three mental health directors, bureaucrats, waitresses, bank officials, journalists and musicians — all say Prangley is one of the most extraordinary and inspiring people they've ever met.
>
> When state officials rave on about him, it begins to sound like something they say to make people think bureaucrats really do care. But members of the old Detroit Film Collective, a group of artists and writers who were anything but bureaucratic are, if anything, even more enthusiastic than the bureaucrats.

In 1990, there was another changing of the guard. State Senate Majority Leader John Engler upset Blanchard in his bid for reelection as governor. Engler chose James Haveman to replace Watkins as Mental Health director. Haveman was executive director of the Grand Rapids–based Bethany Christian Services.

Bethany was a private, nonprofit agency concerned with child welfare, family planning, adoption and refugee services. It had offices in 28 states. From 1978 until 1985, Haveman was director of Kent County's community mental health system. In that role, he showed he was on the same wavelength with Richard in at least one respect: He led the effort away from institutionalization and toward community placement.

Once again, Richard had two new guys to break in — a new governor and a new Mental Health director.

While others in state government hunkered down for the inevitable changing-of-the-guard shake-up, Richard hardly missed a step. His job was secure; his mission, clearly defined. He had no qualms about working with the Republicans.

Registering to vote was one of Richard's first missions as a noninstitutionalized citizen. Back in the early 1970s, when Richard was still living in the Hanson Home, his social worker in Grand Rapids helped him with the voter-registration paperwork. After that, Richard rarely missed an election. As he saw it, being a registered voter helped complete the portrait of the contributing, participating citizen. Richard never got bored with the prospect of having a say in the affairs of his city, state and country.

Richard was neither a Democrat nor a Republican. He simply voted for the person who appealed to him on a personal level. The first president he voted for was Richard Nixon.

Just as he had embraced Milliken (a Republican) and Blanchard (a Democrat), Richard was ready and willing to throw his arms around the Republican from Beal City, Governor-elect John Engler. In fact, more than one person told Richard he bore a resemblance to the new governor, with his oval face, high forehead and fire-hydrant build. Richard was flattered.

Richard was quick to arrange a chat with Engler's Mental Health director, Jim Haveman. And, once again, Richard discovered he was preaching to the choir; the new man in charge already was a believer. Haveman endorsed the philosophy behind the traveling exhibit. He believed that Richard and the other committee members were right in their belief that education was the key to removing the stigma attached to mental illness and developmental disabilities.

During his first three years as Mental Health director, Haveman supported the efforts of the committee. He gave Richard and Tatzmann much of the same leeway Babcock had given them.

Like the four Mental Health directors before him, Haveman quickly took a personal interest in Richard. At first, Haveman was merely intrigued by the mail clerk who seemed to have no reservations about stepping into the director's office and talking about his vision for the department. Quickly, Haveman learned there was a lot more to Richard than the slogans he spouted.

Eventually, Haveman would say that he saw Richard as both a role model and an inspiration. Occasionally, the two men gave speeches together, and Haveman couldn't help but notice that Richard always was the star of the show.

People drew hope for their own lives from Richard's successful struggle. Here was a man who refused to allow a horrible stroke of bad luck beat him down.

With the start of the new decade, the proposed mental health traveling exhibit began to undergo a dramatic technological metamorphosis. In 1992, the board hired a Lansing company called Message Makers to complete the project. Message Makers was an advertising and marketing company that specialized in educating the public about people with disabilities. The company brought the project into the 1990s by turning the exhibit into a computer kiosk. It featured a 30-minute touch-screen program that used cartoon graphics, music and videos to address the stigmas attached to mental disabilities. One of the videos featured Richard in his busboy days at the Pantlind Hotel in Grand Rapids.

The exhibit had its premiere showing in March 1993 at the Conference for Exceptional Children held at the Amway Grand Hotel in Grand Rapids. Naturally, Richard was there for the unveiling. The *Detroit Free Press* covered it. Reporter Patricia Chargot, referring to the video of Richard, wrote: "When Richard Prangley walks into the Amway Grand Hotel in Grand Rapids today, he will see the phantom of a confused young man who could barely cut it as a busboy."

Shortly after the debut, Haveman sent Richard this note:

Dear Richard:

Have I told you that I am tremendously proud of you in what you continue to do for the Department of Mental Health? The completion of the Mental Health Exhibit was great and I look forward to seeing it.

The article in the Detroit Free Press captured things very well, and thanks for being a tremendous advocate for persons who utilize the public mental health system in our state.

My continued best wishes.

On March 29, Haveman sent out a press release announcing that the kiosk would be on display until April 2 in the Mental Health Department, in the Lewis Cass Building in Lansing. From there, the kiosk went on a tour around the state.

As it turned out, that tour was the last gasp in the brief life of the traveling exhibit. Over time, Haveman came to believe the department was investing too much time and too many resources in the exhibit. After all, Mental Health Educational Exhibit Inc. was a nonprofit corporation and not a part of the department.

Haveman became more and more convinced that while the computer kiosk was a step in the right direction, it was, given the possibilities of 1990s technology, too little, too late. It was still a traveling circus in an age of virtual reality. By 1993, computer technology was such that even a traveling computer kiosk seemed archaic, at least as an educational tool. Why lug such a massive chunk of hardware around the state when most schools had their own computers?

In the end, the Department of Mental Health contracted with an organization called Upper Great Lakes Educational Technologies Inc. (UGLETI), a consortium of schools and universities in the Upper Peninsula that put together computer-based educational materials. The UGLETI people reviewed the committee's progress. They considered Richard's goals. They came up with a proposal that, only a few years earlier, would have sounded like an alien language.

In a letter to the Department of Mental Health dated March 27, 1994, Scott Satterlund of UGLETI wrote: "The Mental Health Exhibit project has proceeded to assess the need for the development of a CD-ROM version of the kiosk."

That was it. The evolution of the Mental Health Educational Exhibit was complete.

The CD-ROM discs, under the plan that grew out of UGLETI's proposal, would include study guides. They could be easily distributed to every school in the state, or the country, for that matter, reaching far more children than a static museum exhibit, or even a traveling computer kiosk, could ever hope to reach.

Reaching as many people as possible was, after all, the whole point. Always, the goal of the exhibit was to open minds, particularly *young* minds, to the importance of reaching beyond preconceived notions.

Another thing about a CD-ROM system: The discs could be easily updated as the body of knowledge regarding mental health expanded.

The evolution of Richard's dream, stalled by bureaucracy, then jump-started by technological advances, was complete. In the course of 15 years and $174,000 ($74,000 of it public money; the rest, private money) and an incalculable number of committee meetings, the dream had gone from a permanent museum housed in the administration building at Coldwater to a five-inch plastic disc.

That certainly wasn't the way Richard had envisioned it on that Fourth of July in 1979 when his guardian angel led him to the old administration building at Coldwater and planted an idea that launched a mission. In that moment of revelation, he had imagined a renovated building, bricks and mortar and glass, dedicated to the history of mental health in Michigan.

At first glance, the idea of settling for a plastic disc was disappointing to Richard. But when he stopped to think about it, when he got past the sheer physical contrast between what he had imagined and how it had turned out, the essence of the dream had survived the brutal environment of bureaucracy intact. All along, Richard's only goal had been to deliver a message about the treatment of, and attitudes toward, mental afflictions. He wanted to show what they had been and where they were going.

At its core, Richard's mission was education. A museum seemed like the obvious choice, but he had to admit that taking his message to the people was more efficient and probably, in the end, more effective. And even the false starts hadn't been a total waste. Richard and the project had generated a lot of good publicity. Each step along the way, even the missteps, gave reporters a chance to revisit the Richard Prangley story. Always, he was the true traveling exhibit.

The brochure describing the CD-ROM program, which, incidentally, included a five-minute segment that showed Richard summarizing his life story, described the history of the project this way:

> In 1983, based on the prompting of Richard L. Prangley, a former resident of the Coldwater Regional Center for the Developmentally Disabled, mental health professionals and advocates came together to develop an educational program for the public. The hope was that such a program would eliminate the causes of stigma toward persons with mental illnesses and developmental disabilities.
>
> The original discussions focused on a museum piece, but later evolved into a program that would include a study guide for students and a public exhibit that could be displayed throughout the state. This centered around the theme suggested by Richard Prangley that "People Need People."
>
> Eventually, as a result of Mr. Prangley's idea, it was decided to develop a multimedia unit for classroom instruction in order to reach as many children as possible. The goal of the exhibit is to prove accurate information about mental illness and developmental disabilities, promote understanding and acceptance of persons with these disabilities and thus eliminate the causes of stigma, which limit potential and lessen dignity.

Meanwhile, the reinvention of the educational exhibit ultimately did no damage to Richard's relationship with his boss. Forever the realist, Richard saw no point in harboring any grudges. And for his part, Haveman continued to find in Richard new lessons for a life well lived.

It was, in fact, the example set by Richard that inspired the director to make sure the perspective of the mental health consumer became an official part of the department's perspective. In October 1994, Haveman hired Colleen Jasper to direct the department's newly created Office of Consumer Relations. One of the requirements for the job was a history of mental illness. That was actually part of the job description. Jasper was well qualified. As a result of manic depression, she had been hospitalized 13 times between 1974 and 1985 in private and public institutions.

Soon after she joined the department, Jasper and Richard crossed paths, and the two compared their personal recollections of life in an institution. With the help of medication, therapy and determination, Jasper had been, as she described it, "hospital-free" for nine years when she applied for the Consumer Relations job. Before joining the Department of Mental Health, she worked for an advocacy group called Justice in Mental Health.

In early 1996, Jasper was looking for an assistant. She made it clear that although she would accept an application from anybody, she preferred to hire somebody with a disability.

Haveman made it a point to grill Richard extensively about his experiences both in and out of Coldwater. The director found the stories fascinating, but also informative. His conversations with Richard were, to some extent, research. Haveman always considered the things Richard told him before he took action that would affect those undergoing the same kind of struggles Richard experienced. Haveman said that Richard was a constant reminder of why the Department of Mental Health exists.

In January of 1996, during his annual State of the State address, Governor Engler announced that, beginning that spring, he would combine the Departments of Mental Health and Public Health, along with the Medicaid program, into the Department of Community Health.

When Haveman showed up at work the morning after the speech, Richard was waiting for him outside his office. Richard clearly was in an exuberant, celebratory mood. He offered Haveman a high five. When Haveman asked Richard what he was celebrating, Richard referred to the governor's speech.

Richard said, "We got rid of the stigma word; we're not going to be the Department of *Mental* Health anymore."

Richard Prangley Day

Ever since I was a little boy at Coldwater, all I wanted was to be part of a real family. I thought that maybe once I got out of the institution, my parents would accept me. I thought I could make them understand me. I thought maybe I could be their son again. I'm still hoping for that, but now I have my doubts. They have their lives; I have mine.

— *Richard Prangley*

Gov. John Engler declared June 20, 1995 "Richard Prangley Day" in Michigan. It was the 15th anniversary of Richard's first day on the job with the Department of Mental Health — a significant milestone because it meant that Richard had been working for the department for the same amount of time he was confined to the Coldwater State Home and Training Center.

Fifteen years a victim of the system; 15 years a player in it. There was a reception in the Lewis Cass Building, complete with cake and plenty of sweet words about Richard. Engler praised Richard as "an active advocate for community-based care, one of the cornerstones of Michigan's Community Mental Health System." Two governors, Milliken and Engler, telephoned Richard during the reception.

In a press release issued for the occasion, Haveman was quoted as saying: "This is a milestone in Richard's life, and for the department, as well. Richard's accomplishments in his work and life and his advocacy are powerful illustrations of the abilities that people have and the contributions they can make, despite their disability. Richard is living proof of why it's important to provide as much care as possible in a person's own community, instead of in a state-operated institution."

Working then at the Detroit Center for Charter Schools at Wayne State University, Richard's former boss, Tom Watkins, wrote to Richard on the eve of Richard Prangley Day:

Dear Richard:
If only all employees shared your dedication, work ethic, compassion and commit-

ment, the world would be a much better place. Congratulations on your years of productive service to the citizens of the State of Michigan.

Not only have you performed your job extremely well, you have been a tireless advocate for persons with mental illness and developmental disabilities.

Richard, you were and are an inspiration to me. Many lesser individuals would have let the cruelty you experienced early in life turn them bitter and angry. You channeled your bitterness and anger in a productive fashion and we are all better for knowing you.

Richard, thank you for all you have done to educate the public on mental health issues through the Mental Health Exhibit and your personal actions.
I wish you the very best in the years ahead. You are a very special person.

The Babcocks also wrote:

Dear Richard:

This is a very special day for you, and for all of us.

It gives us a chance to say thank you for over 15 years of hard work, commitment and advocacy for quality mental health services in Michigan.

You have been and continue to be a strong voice for fairness and opportunity for consumers of mental health services, both in your words and in your actions.

We wish we could be with you today. We do want you to know how proud we are to be among your many friends throughout the state.

Congratulations.

Having pursued the exhibit project to its conclusion, Richard settled into his role as a private citizen. Out of the spotlight, he pursued a simple life that revolved around his home and job in the Mental Health Department mailroom.

Although he didn't have to be on the job until 8 a.m., Richard rose each workday precisely at 6 a.m., so he could enjoy an unhurried morning. Richard liked to use those tranquil moments to sit down with his toast and coffee, or shredded wheat with bananas, and simply observe and contemplate his surroundings and belongings.

After showering, Richard sat in his favorite overstuffed chair, greeting the dawn and settling into his successful life. He never took his good fortune for granted; it was a constant source of joy for him.

Dressed in jeans and flannel shirt (a T-shirt in the summer), Richard left his apartment at 7:45 a.m. and walked three city blocks, past houses and state government buildings, to the Lewis Cass Building. The walk, he told anybody who asked, took him nine minutes. Not 10 minutes, but nine minutes.

Early in adulthood, Richard accepted the fact that it was unlikely that he would ever be able to drive a car. Even if he got special permission to take the test orally, driving required too many simultaneous actions, too many quick decisions. He didn't mind. After all, he could walk or ride a bus just about anywhere he wanted to go. And besides, the last thing he needed in his life was a car payment.

On most days, the Mental Health Department's first shipment of mail arrived at 8:15. It was the first of four such shipments in an average day. Richard's first task was to sort the mail and open the envelopes. At 9:30, he piled the mail onto a cart and pushed it through the halls of the Cass Building, delivering the mail to the various offices.

Functionally illiterate, Richard relied on his memory and his knack for recognizing certain configurations of letters. As he delivered the incoming mail, he picked up the outgoing mail, which he then sorted, weighed and prepared for mailing.

Richard almost always ate lunch in one of two cafeterias housed in nearby state office buildings. While some of his coworkers saw the lunch hour as a social occasion, Richard preferred to eat alone. He saw it as a time to collect his thoughts.

A salad or bowl of soup was not Richard's style. He liked full, hot lunches of pork chops, beef and noodles, or chicken, with mashed potatoes, vegetables, and ice cream or pie. Richard spent $6 on a typical lunch.

He found justification for his extravagant lunches on a television health show. As Richard understood it, the nutritionist said that, as people entered their 40s, they had more difficulty burning up calories, particularly in the evening, when they became more sedentary. The message, as Richard interpreted it, was that middle-aged people should eat their largest meal earlier in the day, when they were more active.

Back on the job, Richard also was responsible for maintaining the nine copy machines in the building. He kept them filled with paper and toner. It was his job to order those supplies, as well as other office supplies.

Richard left work each day at 5 p.m. and made the nine-minute walk back to his apartment. At 6 p.m., he turned on his television for the local news, then the national news. It was always NBC and Tom Brokaw. Often, when the weather was decent, Richard went out for dinner, walking to Clara's or to a nearby fast-food restaurant. During winter, he was more inclined to pop a frozen dinner into his oven and eat it while he watched the news. On weekends, he sometimes took the time to prepare a beans-and-franks casserole or macaroni and cheese.

On a typical night, Richard hung around his apartment, arranging and rearranging his collections while listening to Elvis or some other 1950s rocker on radio or compact disc player. Now and then, he liked to spin some vinyl. Often, it was one of the mixed-bag records he bought in the 1970s, records that included songs like Tony Orlando and Dawn's "Knock Three Times," or Norman Greenbaum's "Spirit in the Sky."

Other nights, Richard watched TV, either the standard prime-time net-work programming, a cable channel or one of his rapidly expanding collection of videos. Yes, Richard had spawned still another collection. He never rented movies, he just bought them. If he rented them, he explained to those who asked, then he would have to give them back.

He joined not one video club, but two, and soon had accumulated nearly 300 tapes, including some that perhaps would never find their way into Richard's VCR. Somehow, for example, he had acquired a tape full of *Baywatch* episodes.

Among his favorites: The *Star Wars* trilogy, *Robocop, Towering Inferno, Jurassic Park, Independence Day* and, of course, *Star Trek,* in all its incarnations. More than anything else that turned up on a screen, large or small, Richard loved *Star Trek.* The original series. The *Next Generation.* The movies. He had them all on tape.

When Richard talked about the things he had accomplished in his life, or looked ahead to new challenges, he often borrowed a line from *Star Trek.* Smil-ing at his own audacity, he would say that his goal was "to boldly go where no man has gone."

Star Trek inspired still another collection for Richard: all the space junk that orbited the two television series, as well as the Hollywood treatments.

On Saturdays, Richard sometimes went to movies and restaurants, often with somebody he knew through work. Occasionally, it was the boss himself. Now and then, Mental Health director Haveman took Richard out for Mexican food.

Absent a companion, Richard liked to take the crosstown bus to the mall alone. While there, he typically had dinner at an all-you-can-eat buffet restau-rant, followed by a movie at one of the mall theaters. Richard's friends at work looked up the show times for him in the newspapers.

Richard also liked to cruise flea markets and antique malls, searching for more knickknacks for his ever-expanding collection of collections. Figuring out a way to fit them into his apartment was a constant challenge. He bought them not because he expected them to increase in value, but simply because he liked them.

Well-meaning people often told Richard he ought to get a pet — a cat, per-haps, or a parakeet — to keep him company. But the large ceramic cat that crouched on the carpet of Richard's living room, the one that required no food or shots or weekend shelter when Richard went away, suited Richard just fine. He even preferred artificial plants over real ones.

Richard was constantly torn between his desire for what he called "nice things" and his long-range dream of buying a house. The more he settled into his niche as a homebody, the more Richard dreamed of a lawn to mow, a gar-den to tend and a garage where he could set up a woodworking shop. It was a dream that would require a hefty down payment.

Around 1990, Richard was closing in on that goal. By paying only $200 per month for the lower half of the house near downtown Lansing, and by living frugally, Richard managed to accumulate nearly $10,000 in his savings account at Old Kent Bank.

Then Richard learned a hard lesson about the perils of making financial investments based on vague promises. Because the homeowner told Richard he could buy the house some day, he began sinking his own money into the place. He bought paint and lumber, fencing and shrubs, hardware and flooring. Richard even bought a power mower. Why not? The house would be his one day. He thought he might as well start fixing it up.

But the owner died suddenly, and her heir didn't share her view of the future. Of course, Richard had no legal claim, neither to the house, nor to the improvements he made. Not only did Richard never get a chance to buy the house, but his precarious relationship with the new owner eventually forced him to move. His investment had come to nothing.

Discouraged that his chance at home ownership had disappeared, Richard decided that maybe, after all, it was an unrealistic goal. He became a free-spender once again, buying furniture and electronics for his new apartment: a new television and stereo system and an easy chair from which to enjoy them. He began indulging all his whims again, buying every knickknack, compact disc and video cassette that caught his eye.

By 1997, Richard's savings amounted to $5, the minimum required to keep an account at the State Employees Credit Union. He was staying afloat financially, but just barely.

Richard was earning about $12 per hour at the time. He got paid every two weeks. Minus taxes and other deductions, his paycheck amounted to about $737. His rent, $480 per month, plus utilities, took a substantial bite out of his income, but he had few other obligations, except for the ones that resulted from his conspicuous consumerism.

Richard had seven credit cards. On the defensive, he explained that he never *set out* to own seven credit cards. They just kept coming in the mail, and Richard just kept using them to pay for meals, to pay for videos and compact discs, to cover his Christmas shopping and just about any other miscellaneous expense. The plastic came in handy, he said, in those moments at the mall when he saw something he just couldn't resist.

Richard never acknowledged that his spending was a problem, only that it was something he had to "bring under control," at least until he found a way to earn more money.

Meanwhile, he continued to invest a healthy chunk of income in entertainment, including restaurants, movies and his main hobby; acquiring things. He also liked an occasional adventure. He especially liked amusement parks. Once or twice each summer, friends took him to Michigan's Adventure, in Muskegon, where Richard generally stuck to the milder rides.

One summer, he took a bus to Cedar Point in Sandusky, Ohio. He made the trip alone. Richard had seen the TV ads for a ride called the Demon Drop, and he had made up his mind to give it a try. He lived to tell about it, but decided after that to stay with the Ferris wheels and carousels.

Richard's experience in California didn't douse his wanderlust altogether. It was back in the 1980s, shortly after he moved to Lansing, that Richard was struck by the desire to see what life might be like in another country. He remembered hearing that a person could go from Detroit to Canada without too much trouble. One weekend, Richard took a bus to Detroit, then crossed over into Windsor, Ontario. Richard discovered, of course, that life in Canada looks a lot like life in the United States. But the money sure looked different. Plus, it was fun to say he had visited another country.

Richard made a half-dozen trips to Windsor in the following years. Eventually he learned, strictly by accident, that Windsor held an attraction that somehow had eluded his attention: a casino. Naturally, Richard had to take a look inside.

The bright lights and busy clatter of the place appealed to Richard. He asked lots of questions and quickly mastered the technique of feeding $1 tokens into the slot machines. He walked out of the casino $95 ahead that day. However, with all those Canadian souvenirs lying in wait for Richard between the casino and the Ambassador Bridge, the winnings never made it back to Lansing.

Richard returned to the casino two months later, but he was unable to repeat the beginner's luck of the first trip. He went home determined to have another go at it, and maybe someday try his luck in Las Vegas.

In 1992, Richard, at 42, set his sights on his most ambitious trip since Los Angeles. Purposely avoiding the flea markets and antique shops for a few months, he managed to save a substantial sum of money. That summer, he boarded a train in Lansing alone and rode it to Florida.

Richard had high hopes for the trip, not only because he was going to Disney World, but also because he looked forward to spending some time with his parents and older sister, all of whom lived in New Smyrna Beach, Florida.

Again, Richard's vision of a joyful reunion never materialized. He spent three awkward days with his parents and his sister. They were cordial enough toward him, but to Richard, his parents seemed tense and uncomfortable. Clearly, they took no joy in the reunion. After three days of strained civility, Richard and his sister made the one-hour trip by car to Disney World, in Orlando.

From the beginning, Richard and his sister were on a collision course. She didn't approve of Richard's extravagant spending habits, particularly his insatiable craving for what she considered tacky and over-priced souvenirs, and she told him so. As Richard saw it, the money was his and he had the right to spend it any way he chose. He believed his sister was jealous because he had the luxury of spending freely, while she was forced to economize. Richard, who paid her way into the park, thought she should be grateful, instead of critical.

The dispute came to a head over a backpack. Eventually, Richard needed something with which to haul the $400 worth of Disney World souvenirs he had accumulated. He settled on a souvenir backpack. Again, his sister rolled her eyes. The thing was outrageously priced. She had witnessed enough. She told Richard that he was out of control, that he was foolish.

Richard also had had enough. He reminded her that the money was his, after all. He had earned it. How he chose to spend it was his business, and his alone. He accused his sister of resenting his success and, in fact, envying it.

Richard and his sister parted company at the hotel. She went back to New Smyrna Beach, and Richard continued to stuff his new backpack with the things that pleased him, buying them with money he had earned. His sister returned to Disney World a few days later to retrieve Richard. They apologized to each other and returned to New Smyrna Beach together. The next day, after some stiff hugs and vague promises to do it again someday, Richard caught a flight home.

Back in Lansing, Richard continued to look for a surrogate family. In the spring of 1996, he found the next best thing: a baseball team.

Richard never showed much of an interest in sports until the fall of 1995, when construction began on Oldsmobile Park, the new home of the Lansing Lugnuts, a minor-league affiliate of the Kansas City Royals. The Lugnuts, formerly the Sultans of Springfield, Illinois, opened the 1996 season in Lansing.

This captured Richard's imagination, partly because playing baseball in the courtyard at Coldwater was one of the few joys he knew in the institution, but mostly because Richard knew his apartment was within walking distance of Oldsmobile Park. In fact, Richard could leave the ballpark and walk a few blocks down Michigan Avenue and he'd be at his home-away-from-home, Clara's restaurant. A home-town baseball team was something Richard could become a part of, something he could pursue all summer long. Richard became a Lugnuts booster when Oldsmobile Park was still a hole in the frozen ground.

On the late-winter Saturday when tickets for individual games went on sale, Richard got up early enough to catch a bus to the Lansing Mall and take his position in line by 7 a.m. He was by no means the earliest of the birds. Richard stood in line for five hours. He bought tickets for the first three games of the season. Richard had no trouble passing the time in line. Although he already had spent $300 on Lugnuts paraphernalia before that day, he bought another armload of stuff before the wait was over. When he wasn't buying, he was talking, making conversation with others in line.

One of them, a woman from the nearby town of Grand Ledge named Julie, was so impressed with Richard that she called the *State Journal* eager to tell

somebody about her encounter with a man who reminded her so much of For-
rest Gump, a character in a movie that was popular at the time.

"I didn't stop thinking about him all weekend," Julie told a reporter. "What
a great outlook. What an enthusiasm for life. He can teach people a lot. He
made me realize that it's not so much the circumstances of your life, but what
you do with them. Sometimes the world is so cynical. When I was done visiting with him, I felt so optimistic."

Richard had a knack for striking up casual conversations with strangers, and
sometimes those conversations developed into casual relationships. In a ticket
line, or at the ballpark itself, Richard talked baseball, all the time working his
way into the family of Lugnuts fans.

In the summer of 1996, Richard went to 45 Lugnuts games, two-thirds of
the home-game schedule. He ate Polish sausage. He learned the words to the
Lugnuts song and sang as loud as anybody. The attendants began to recognize
and greet him, as did the other ballpark regulars. It made Richard feel like he
was part of something.

But then the end of the season came and Richard had to turn elsewhere.

That fall, he turned to Mt. Hope Church, a flashy, theatrical, nondenomi-
national megachurch on Lansing's west side. Richard learned about the church
through some fellow state employees who were members and started going to
services in late September.

Mt. Hope Church was anything but modest in its approach to worship. It
had a 3,000-seat sanctuary-auditorium in which it held Sunday services and
staged flashy productions with names like "America: The Dream That Never
Dies." In 1994, the ever-expanding church added a 76,000-square-foot, $4.5-
million prayer chapel.

Sunday services were, in the words of a *Lansing State Journal* article, "high-
tech tent revivals … [spreading] … fundamentalist Christianity of the '90s,
choreographed and marketed like a Broadway musical."

But the church wasn't so big, or so flashy, that the leaders forgot their fundamental mission to recruit new members. A church van made the rounds each
Sunday morning, picking up people who wanted to come to services but didn't
have a way to get there.

Richard sometimes rode the shuttle on Sunday mornings, but he preferred
the Sunday night services, which were generally more theatrical. Sometimes a
member of the church gave him a lift. Sometimes he rode the bus. He liked to
stay after services and hang around the fellowship, where he'd strike up a conversation or two, always hoping to make a connection.

As always, Richard recruited more admirers. Once people learned Richard's
history and saw what he had made of himself, they couldn't help but admire and
respect him. But Richard wanted more than respect; he wanted love.

On the surface, Richard wasn't particularly lonely. He truly liked living alone. He enjoyed the freedom and peace it gave him. At Coldwater, Richard had neither privacy nor freedom. As an independent middle-aged man, he had both. Richard's loneliness went deeper than that. It was a profound hunger to be intimately connected to other human beings. Always, Richard was looking for the family he never had.

As for romance, Richard never thought much about it. Somehow he arrived at the conclusion, without ever articulating it, not even to himself, that, like driving, it just wasn't in the cards for him. Locked up in Coldwater, Richard never learned about the opposite sex at the time in his life when he should have. Perhaps he just didn't have the intellectual and emotional tools to initiate and sustain an intimate relationship.

In any case, by middle age the window of opportunity slammed shut. Richard was left without a clue about how to relate to women in an intimate way. He wasn't even interested in learning. Like driving, it was just too complicated, too much of a mystery. To Richard, women were like the people on the streets of Los Angeles who spoke a different language.

Sex was another alien concept to Richard. Except for what happened in Coldwater and images that turned up in some of the action movies he liked, Richard had no experience. Even in middle age, he knew incredibly little about sexual attraction and all it implied.

In 1994, he struck up a friendship with a young man who worked as an intern in the Department of Mental Health. The two men went out to movies together and shared an occasional dinner at a restaurant. As time passed, Richard noticed that his friend seemed to have less and less time for him. When Richard asked him why that was so, his friend explained that he and his wife were expecting their first child and that he was spending more time with his wife.

Richard truly didn't understand the connection. He could see why his friend might have less free time *after* he got his baby. But why *before* the baby came? At age 45, after all he had accomplished, Richard thought that babies literally came from hospitals. He thought that when young couples were ready to start their families, they went to the hospital and picked out their babies in much the same way they selected their dining room sets or their refrigerators.

In the course of a conversation with Richard about his friend's growing aloofness, Manfred Tatzmann realized that Richard had no understanding of human reproduction. Tatzmann got some books and had "the talk" with Richard — about 30 years too late.

As for Richard's relationship with God, it remained steady over the years, regardless of what church he happened to be attending. On one of the walls of his living room, Richard displayed a large, framed likeness of Jesus, which he got at an antique shop. He said it reminded him of the painting that hung in the dining room in his house in Jenison — the one he saw for the last time when he was 6 years old.

On another wall of his living room, there was a crucifix, accompanied by two plaques bearing biblical verses:

> And we know that all things work together for good to them who love God, to them who are called according to His purpose.
>
> — Romans 8:28

> "Choose you this day whom ye will serve, but as for me and my house we will serve the Lord."
>
> — Joshua 24:15

Throughout his life, Richard remained convinced that divine intervention played a key role in his success, in big ways and small. It turned him in the right direction when he was lost and afraid on an unfamiliar city street. It led him to strangers inclined to help him. It helped him invent ways to compensate for his illiteracy. It helped him resist the bitterness and hopelessness that might have consumed him. Richard said that sometimes he literally felt a hand on his shoulder, gently guiding him through life, nudging him in the right direction.

Richard always considered himself an exception, one of the lucky ones. Occasionally, he ran into former fellow residents of Coldwater. Rarely were they leading lives that could be considered successful, at least in conventional terms. Sometimes they held menial jobs, or temporary jobs for which they were paid in cash, under the table. But usually, they had no jobs at all. They limped along on public assistance. The dismal lack of success surprised Richard, particularly when it was somebody who was known as a good worker inside the institution, a person recognized by everybody as someone on the ball. Sometimes it was a person Richard had envied.

Richard spent a lot of time thinking about the difference between himself and the drifters, the men who lacked the desire to determine their own destiny. He tried to analyze it, to distill the ingredient that made one man keep trying, while others gave up. It wasn't intelligence, nor was it a simple willingness to work. The way Richard had it figured, it was a refusal to be consumed by bitterness or apathy.

It wasn't that Richard didn't *feel* bitter on the day he walked out of Coldwater. It wasn't that he was able to forget the fact that he was a victim of a terrible injustice. It was just that he refused to let the injustice control the rest of his life.

The others surrendered to their bitterness. They were hostile, or they were passive, unable to muster the effort to take control of their lives. Richard understood why they felt that way. But he also understood that the surrender only perpetuated the injustice. For whatever reason, something he was born with, or something that grew inside him, Richard refused to make a career out of being a victim.

One summer day, long after Richard had established himself as a solid citizen and mental health crusader, he crossed paths with a man who had been considered one of the brightest lights of Cottage 12 during the time Richard was living there. Richard was walking down Martin Luther King Boulevard in Lansing that day, on his way to a bus stop. Suddenly, there was the man, rummaging through a trash can out in front of a service station.

Richard approached the man and greeted him. He recognized Richard, but couldn't remember his name. Richard refreshed his memory. The two men shared some memories of Cottage 12 and the institution in general. Eventually, the talk turned to life after Coldwater, and Richard asked him what he was doing for a living. He said he wasn't doing anything, that he was on public assistance.

The man never asked Richard about his life, but Richard volunteered the information. He told him about his job, his apartment and his work as an advocate for mental health. Then Richard asked him if he would be interested in working with him in the Mental Health Department mailroom. Richard wasn't sure he would have any influence in getting somebody else a job in the department, but he was willing to give it a try. But the man told Richard he wasn't interested.

The man dodged Richard's question about where he was living and how he filled his days. In fact, once the conversation moved beyond the memories of Coldwater, he didn't have much to say. After several unsuccessful attempts to engage the man in conversation, Richard gave up. With hardly a good-bye, the two men went their separate ways.

Richard caught his bus. As it pulled away from the curb, he looked through the window, back at the man, who was digging through the trash again. Richard felt sorry for him. One more person defeated by the system.

Richard pretty much had the system figured out, with one excrutiating exception: his relationship with his family. Despite the sporadic attempts over the years to gloss over the past, the old wounds had never quite healed. In fact, they had never even *begun* to heal. In middle age, Richard felt no closer to reconciliation with his parents than on the day he walked out of the institution. The truth was that the bonds between Richard and the other members of his family, the bonds that Richard had always dreamed of reestablishing, never had been established in the first place.

Family ties come from shared experiences, from memories and inside jokes and secrets, and the fact remained that Richard was never a part of the Prangley-family lore. Richard was the occasional blip on the screen. The Prangley family was a family of 12. Richard was always number 13.

Now and then, one of Richard's siblings acknowledged the estrangement. The brother who was born six years after Richard, once said: "I knew I had another brother, but I never knew him as a brother. I feel bad that I lost him for so many years."

But most of the time, Richard's brothers and sisters were circling the wagons around their parents, shielding them from a brother who, from their point of view, seemed determined to hurt John and Dorothy Prangley. As they saw it, they *tried* to be nice to Richard. They even attempted, now and then, to consider Richard part of the family. But, from their perspective, Richard's celebrated desire for healing didn't seem sincere. If Richard wasn't spouting his platitudes about mental health reform, he was telling horror stories about Coldwater. It was bad enough at family gatherings; worse yet in public.

The way the siblings saw it, Richard seemed bound and determined to cast his parents as villains and himself as a victim of their carelessness. He did it in the newspapers and on television. Then one day he started talking about a book. He was going to collaborate on a book about his life, including all the unpleasantness at Coldwater. Richard was going to tell it all — again. This time in greater detail. He encouraged his parents and some of his siblings to participate, to help tell the Richard Prangley story from their point of view. Except for one brother, they declined. They told Richard that he should stop living in the past.

This created in Richard a powerful conflict. One day he was on fire with a determination to tell the truth; the next he was terrified that more public disclosure might further offend his parents and spoil, once and for all, his chances for rejoining the family — a dream he could never quite bring himself to abandon.

Richard's brother, who was 10 years younger than him, died of a diabetes-related illness in December 1995. All 12 surviving Prangleys converged in Grand Rapids for the funeral. It was the first complete family gathering since the awkward dinner at the home of Richard's parents in Grandville shortly after Richard was released from Coldwater.

Richard realized that the funeral was a somber occasion, but he couldn't resist hoping that it would be the family gathering of his dreams. Maybe this shared tragedy, this bond of sorrow over his brother's death, would do what nothing else had. Maybe it would be Richard's official entry into the family. But like a lot of Richard's fantasies regarding his family, this one came up short.

At the funeral, Richard felt more like a friend of the family than a member of it. Some of Richard's siblings still clearly resented his success and the way he had handled it. The fact remained that Richard had hurt John and Dorothy Prangley with so many of his public outpourings. Now he was talking about doing a book, a book that would make the Prangleys look bad all over again. And then he had the nerve to ask John and Dorothy to participate.

Only well into middle age did Richard acknowledge the truth that was getting harder and harder to deny:

"They've got their lives to live, and I've got my life to live," he said. "They don't want to be bothered with my life. They never have. I think I still make my mother nervous."

Yet, Richard would never abandon his attempt to make his life mesh with the lives of his parents. He constantly walked a tightrope between hoping for a miracle and giving up.

One Christmas Eve, long after he began to accept the possibility that he would never be reunited with his parents in any meaningful sense, Richard, on an impulse, made a telephone call to his parents' home in Florida, to wish them Merry Christmas.

The previous year had not been a particularly good one for the relationship between Richard and his parents. John and Dorothy knew the book was coming. Judging from all of Richard's previous declarations, the Prangleys knew they once again would be painted as villains. They wanted him to drop the project.

But it was Christmas, a time when hearts were supposed to be a little softer. He chatted with his mother, then asked to speak to his father, who was too busy at the moment to come to the telephone. Richard's mother told him that his father would call him back. Richard stayed in his apartment all night, listening to Christmas music and waiting for the telephone call. He couldn't help but think of the 15 Christmas Eves and Christmas mornings spent inside the institution. He remembered the hard candy packed inside the empty toilet paper rolls. He remembered watching the other kids leave, one by one. He remembered wondering why he couldn't go home, too.

Christmas morning came and went. Richard's telephone never rang.

Surely his dad would call Christmas Day. If not, than maybe on New Year's Day. Or perhaps he'd call once the hubbub of the holidays were over. Like everybody else, Richard had his low points, but he always found a way to avoid despair. It was a survival mechanism, and Richard was, above all, a survivor.

He had been deposited, at age 6, at the mouth of a dark tunnel. When he was 21, he stumbled out into the light, rubbing his eyes, profoundly disoriented. He had spent 15 years, the *formative* years as they're called, forming nothing more than a strategy of how to survive inside an institution.

Inside Coldwater, Richard never learned the multiplication tables or the alphabet or the names of the state capitals. But he missed out on more than just those things that come from books. He never knew a carefree childhood, or the experimentation of adolescence. He never learned how to swim or ride a bike or shoot a slingshot or fold a paper airplane.

Richard never slept in the top bunk of a bunk bed. He never caught fireflies in a jar. He never knew the excitement of a Friday-night football game, or the tenderness of a good-night kiss. He never sat in a field under a night sky with a friend and traded speculations on the mysteries of the universe. He never tasted a s'more, that camping favorite created by toasting a marshmallow over a campfire, then squishing the gooey, warm marshmallow between two graham crackers with chocolate in the middle.

For some of the missed opportunities, the windows slammed shut forever. In his 40s, after too many skinned elbows and mouthfuls of pool water, Richard gave up on trying to master the mysteries of bike riding and swimming. He told himself he would have to live out his life without those skills. As for the rest of the life lessons swallowed up in the 15-year gap, the ones within his grasp, Richard had a lot of catching up to do. He was the first one to say so.

He had his first s'more when he was 47. One August night, he sat at a bonfire on a Lake Huron beach and, following the instruction of his host, built one of the campfire delicacies. He ate it. Then he made and ate six more. When one of his companions commented on Richard's appetite, he explained that, as a child, he had missed out on the s'more experience and was making up for lost time. It was too dark for anybody to see Richard's sly smile spread, the one that crept over his face whenever he realized, to his own delighted surprise, that he created a genuine joke.

By the time he tasted his first s'more, Richard's dark, closely cropped hair was graying at the temples. His lanky adolescent body had taken on a typical middle-age spread. Richard's tendency to slouch his shoulders made him look like he was perpetually ducking something, a legacy, perhaps, of the institution, as was his shuffling gate.

Richard's pale green eyes never lost their tendency to dart around a room, as if scanning the terrain for the trouble that was sure to come. Richard was constantly sizing up the people who were sizing up him.

The physical package — sagging shoulders, nervous eyes and hesitant gait — broadcast a lack of self-confidence. It was a false message. Although Richard encountered people who looked down on him, Richard genuinely believed that was result of their shortcomings, not his.

Self-confidence? Richard's occasionally reached epic proportions.

Once, as a joke, a man suggested to Richard that, in light of all his accomplishments, he deserved to have his face on a postage stamp. That very day, Richard went to Gov. John Engler's office and asked how, exactly, a person could achieve that goal. One of the governor's aides told Richard he would have to make his pitch to the U.S. Congress. Richard got a list of Michigan's U.S. senators and representatives. He was about to launch another of his letter-writing blitzes when a friend suggested, as gently as possible, that perhaps the man was joking about the stamp.

Maybe so, Richard said, but it was still a good idea.

If Elvis was worthy, why not Richard?

On a less-ambitious scale, Richard thought he deserved a job promotion. He liked most of his duties in the mailroom but began to resent others, particularly the "grunt" jobs, like moving heavy metal desks and file cabinets from floor to floor. As a young man, he didn't mind the heavy lifting so much, but in middle age and after 16 years of muscle work, he had grown weary of that aspect of the job. Also he couldn't help but feel that he had risen above moving furniture.

On good days, Richard took comfort in the fact that the job was secure and the pay was decent. On bad days, he felt bored and restless. He saw himself on the verge of change. Richard dared to dream about turning his avocation into a vocation and becoming a full-time advocate for the developmentally disabled. The truth was, he saw himself in public relations as an ambassador for the Community Health Department.

That was one of the topics Richard liked to think about on his long summer-evening walks. Stopping occasionally to ponder the moon and the stars, he wondered about his place in the universe. Richard was convinced, more and more, that his role was to deliver a message, a message of tolerance, of withholding judgment, of taking time to find the value in every human being.

Richard loved the night sky. He loved the mystery of it, the prospect of endless galaxies, different worlds. Maybe somewhere among the infinite possibilities, a world existed where people were defined not by their limitations, but by their potential.

Colophon

*Type was set in 11-point Garamond on 13-point leading.
This book was produced by Aaron Phipps
with a Power Macintosh 7100/66 computer using
Quark XPress 3.31. The photos were
digitally processed with
Adobe Photoshop 4.0 software.
Film of the electronic pages was accomplished by
Electronic Publishing center.*

✝